the prodigy

exit the underground

First published in Great Britain in 1996 by Virgin Books

332 Ladbroke Grove
London
W10 5AH

atalogue record for this book is available from the British Library

0 7535 00639

the prodigy

exit the underground

the prodigy

exit the underground

lisa verrico

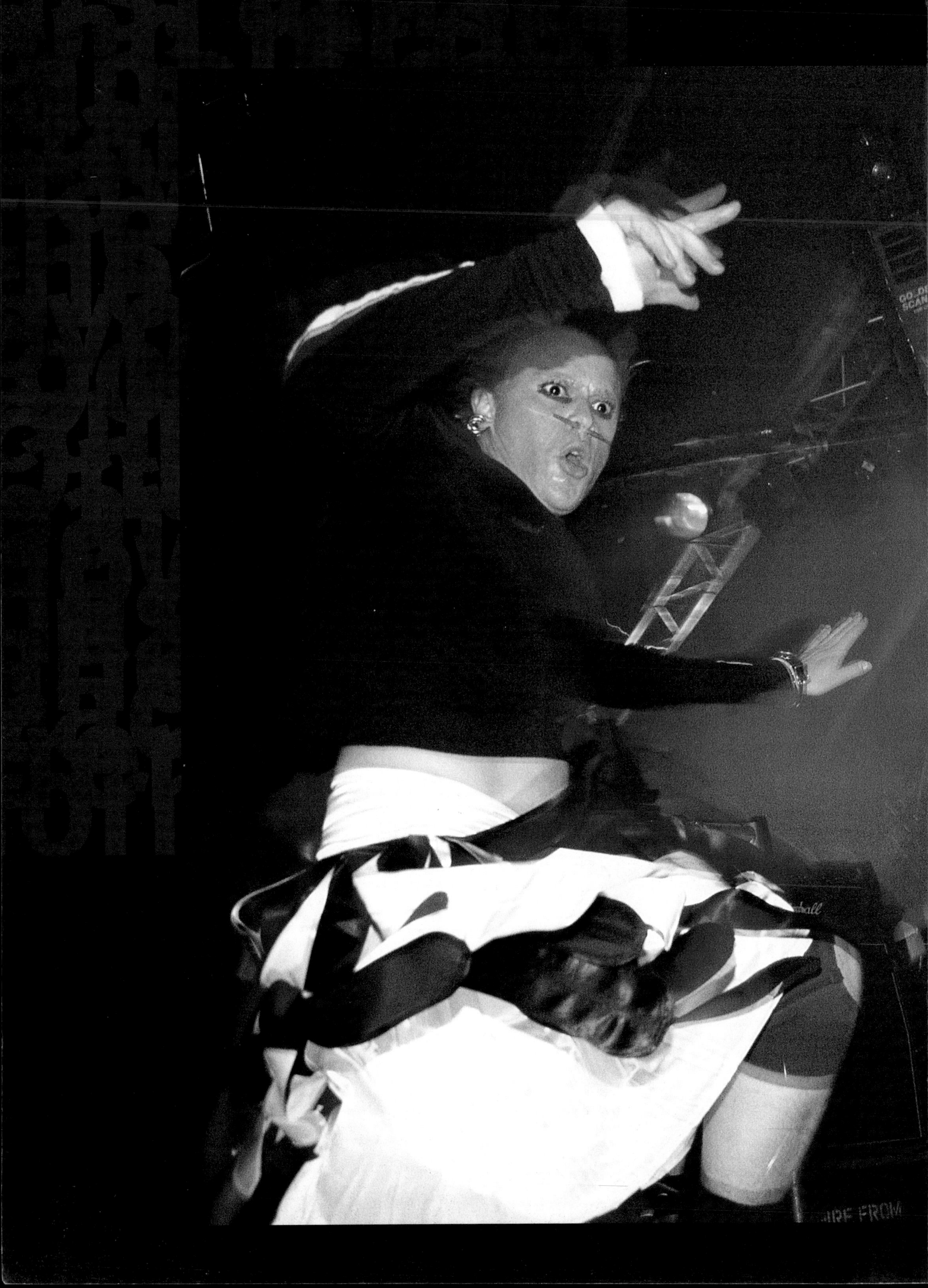

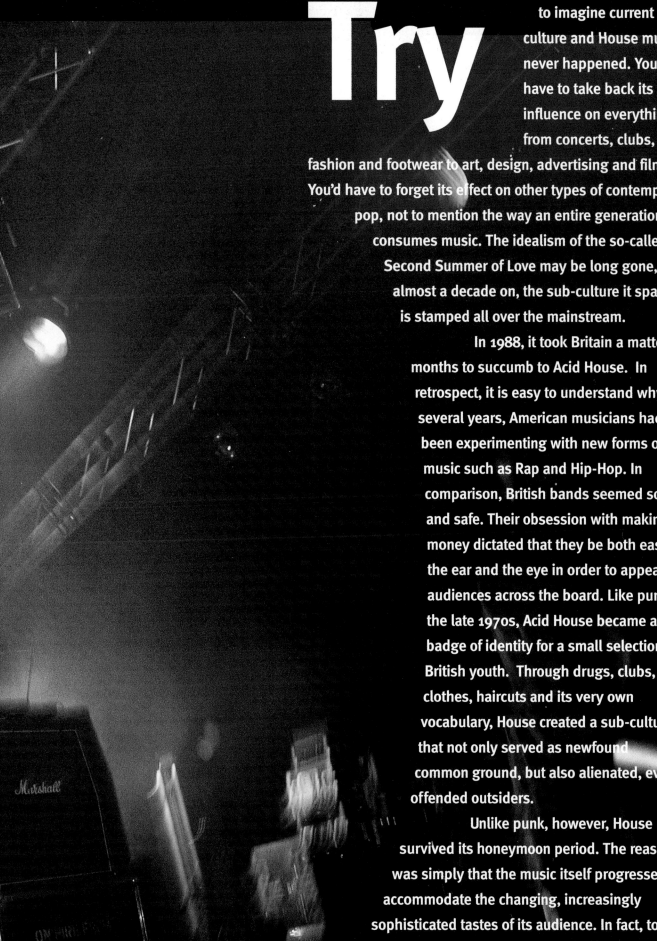

Try

to imagine current youth culture and House music never happened. You'd have to take back its influence on everything from concerts, clubs, fashion and footwear to art, design, advertising and film. You'd have to forget its effect on other types of contemporary pop, not to mention the way an entire generation now consumes music. The idealism of the so-called Second Summer of Love may be long gone, but almost a decade on, the sub-culture it spawned is stamped all over the mainstream.

In 1988, it took Britain a matter of months to succumb to Acid House. In retrospect, it is easy to understand why. For several years, American musicians had been experimenting with new forms of music such as Rap and Hip-Hop. In comparison, British bands seemed soft and safe. Their obsession with making money dictated that they be both easy on the ear and the eye in order to appeal to audiences across the board. Like punk in the late 1970s, Acid House became a badge of identity for a small selection of British youth. Through drugs, clubs, clothes, haircuts and its very own vocabulary, House created a sub-culture that not only served as newfound common ground, but also alienated, even offended outsiders.

Unlike punk, however, House survived its honeymoon period. The reason was simply that the music itself progressed to accommodate the changing, increasingly sophisticated tastes of its audience. In fact, today, cutting-edge dance music – with its rock, Dub, Hip-Hop and heavy metal influences – bares scant resemblance to its melodic House origins.

Dozens of DJs, artists and record labels can claim to have played their part in the evolution of 1990s dance culture. Only one band, however, has stayed ahead of each new trend. Since forming in the rave days of 1990, Essex-based The Prodigy have mixed up musical styles, absorbed myriad influences and experimented with new technology in order to keep dance music on the move. More than any other artist, they have proved that dance acts can compete with conventional rock bands both in terms of album sales and live shows.

Significantly, The Prodigy have reached their current (1996) position as Europe's biggest-selling alternative dance act without ever compromising either their music or their attitude. In February 1996, fashion finally caught up with the band when Firestarter, the first single from their third album, entered the UK charts at No. 1.

Exit the Underground is the tale of how that happened.

chapter one

Slap

bang in the summer of 1991, The Prodigy's first hit single split musical opinion as much as any Sex Pistols song ever had before it. Charly, a manic, bass-heavy mix of breakbeats, Techno, frantic samples and a snippet of speech about a cartoon cat, was either the most unlistenable, least intelligent novelty record of the decade to date, or a skilfully constructed,

cheekily innovative hardcore anthem. As a musical sign of the times, there was no doubt that Charly was spot on. The song reflected not only the crazed, Ecstasy-infested sound of the rave records that had inspired its creator, 19-year-old Liam Howlett, but also captured the energy and intensity of the rave scene itself. "The Prodigy," said Liam Howlett at the time of the record's release, "is all about getting the buzz of a rave on to vinyl."

Charly climbed to No. 3 in the UK singles chart (it topped the dance chart for weeks), eventually sold more than 300,000 copies and kicked off The Prodigy's hugely successful commercial career. It also began not only the band's long-term struggle to retain their underground credibility, but also an uneasy relationship with the media – both of which have intensified over the years.

Although The Prodigy's music quickly progressed beyond rave (the band now claim to hate the term), to understand the attitude with which they still approach every aspect of being in a band

"The Prodigy is all about getting the **buzz** of a rave on to vinyl" – Liam

"The last thing I **want is for The Prodigy** to be a one-hit wonder" — Liam

"A lot of my friends have told me that they think Charly will get into the Top 40. I hope they're wrong" – Liam

Liam Howlett

Maxim Reality

Leeroy Thornhill

Keith Flint

(from making records and playing live to dealing with their public image and their attitude to fans), it is important to understand the mentality of the scene from which they emerged. The Prodigy's strict sense of integrity (they won't play on TV, won't get involved in publicity stunts and won't compromise their performance or their appearance in order to broaden their appeal) is simply their attempt to stay loyal to the ethos of the original rave scene.

What was actually Acid House on a massive scale, raves took off in the UK at the end of the 1980s. Huge illegal warehouse parties and outdoor gatherings – attracting tens of thousands of people – turned a rapidly growing number of the country's youth on to a new form of music played entirely by machines. Acid House was a relentless, minimalist, manic offshoot of the House and Techno scenes that had developed in the North American cities of Chicago and Detroit. With a name thought to have originated from the group Phuture's Acid Trax single of 1987, Acid House was characterised by hypnotic rhythms, offbeat soundscapes and weird samples. To intensify the music's mind-altering frequencies, the melodies central to American House were omitted. Acid was more extreme, almost alien. The beats were impossibly fast – far too fast ever to be recreated by real musicians – and the sounds were certainly not human.

The explosion in awareness, production and consumption of the chemical MDMA – ie the recreational drug Ecstasy – that happened at the same time as Acid House was no coincidence. The incessant, repetitive beat of the man-made music helped Ecstasy users to maintain both their energy levels and a trance-like state in which they could dance non-stop for hours on end. The loved-up, hedonistic Ecstasy experience led the rave scene to adopt a recycled Hippie mantra from the 1960s. 1988 became known as the Second Summer of Love, smiley T-shirts and baggy jeans became street fashion and alcohol was snubbed in favour of high-energy, non-alcoholic herbal and caffeine cocktails.

Naturally, the connection between the rave scene and drugs caused the authorities to try to intervene. As they began steps to criminalise the massive parties, however, pirate-radio stations sprung up in order not only to play the latest new music, but also to provide information on where and when events were taking place. Innovatively designed, often humorous flyers, available only from a small, select number of outlets, would also carry necessary

names, dates or telephone numbers. Naturally, the rebellious, underground element only added to the attraction for ravers.

For the future members of The Prodigy, there was one further important aspect to the rave scene. Due to their scale, many of the events were, inevitably, happening out in the countryside. In the southeast of England, service stations on the M25 motorway consequently became meeting places for carloads of partygoers. The motorway cut off a section of southwestern Essex that became a haven for the raves, and, subsequently, produced a substantial number of bands, record labels and dance DJs.

"A lot of my friends have told me that they think Charly will get into the top 40," said Liam Howlett, just days before the record entered the Top 10, in The Prodigy's first-ever press interview with Melody Maker. "I hope they're wrong. It's not that I don't ever want to be successful, it's just that I'd rather continue to be an underground act for another two or three records and work on expanding a hardcore following. The reason so many dance groups are sitting in the charts one week and then completely

forgotten the next is because they have no real foundation. The last thing I want is for The Prodigy to be a one-hit wonder."

Whether fortunate or unfortunate, Howlett got into making rave records just as the scene was about to erupt. Rave had survived for three years underground, but the sheer volume of people now involved meant that something had to give.

Indeed, for at least the previous 12 months, large-scale events had been taken over almost entirely by commercially minded promoters, interested purely in earning money by selling out the scene at the highest possible profit margin.

"We knew Charly would be big on the rave scene," said Liam, "because that was our thing. We were so into raving that we knew exactly what people wanted. But I didn't write it as a commercial song. When it charted, I was totally shocked. We didn't really know what to make of it because it was something we had never looked for. Almost immediately, we wondered if we had made a wrong move, but ultimately we knew we were true to ourselves and to the scene."

Other people, however, didn't view Charly in the same light. Despite the musical credibility of the song itself, The Prodigy were

accused of exploiting rave. A few other acts from the same background, such as Adamski, Shades of Rhythm and N-Joi, had already experienced minor chart success, but nothing like Charly. It was, without doubt, the record that rode the rave wave overground.

In retrospect, however, any single that had caught the attention of the entire underground the way that Charly had at that time would have enjoyed the same level of success. It was all a question of logistics. The number of punters into rave simply started to surpass the number of records required to take a song to the top of the national charts. "I didn't write Charly to get on the telly," insisted Liam. "People say it was commercial because it sold so many copies." Charly sold this number of copies for several reasons – for one, the "Charly says..." sample was so distinctive that it made the record stand out both at raves and on the radio. Also, The Prodigy had been PA-ing the song in their set for six months prior to its release. They calculated that more than 50,000 people had seen the song played live before it was ever in the shops. Moreover, even at that early stage, the band's live show was head and shoulders above the bulk of other dance acts, which attracted more attention to the tunes the band were playing.

Consequently, the volume of pre-release interest in Charly was phenomenal. In fact, The Prodigy's record label was getting dozens of phone calls from record shops and pirate-radio stations before Liam had even mastered the tape. Charly have been written just before Christmas the previous year, 1990, in one of Liam's by then regular post-party writing sessions. He had come home, turned on the television and seen a 1970s, government-produced children's safety ad, featuring a cartoon cat called Charly. The young boy in the advert translates the cat's miaow into: "Charly says, never go out without telling your mummy first." Liam thought it was hilarious and figured that if he sampled the boy's voice over a hard tune, it would be both a new musical angle and an interesting experiment. He tuned into the same channel at the same time the following week to tape the extract he wanted. He would later be sued – unsuccessfully – for doing so. The very first version of Charly had a heavy Ragga bassline running through it, but Liam later decided to remix it to put out as a single, in order to make it more danceable.

Significantly, as soon as it came out on promo, the tune was picked up by all the major underground DJs in the country. Later, when Charly went mainstream, it was, inevitably, shunned by the élitist clubs and DJs. That was expected. What wasn't, however, was the rush by rave outsiders to cash in on Charly's success. The single was such a significant hit that it quickly became the catalyst for dozens of crap, exploitative copies. The most successful of these were Shaft's Roobarb and Custard, Urban Hype's Trip to Trumpton and The Smarties' Sesame's Treet, which actually reached No. 1. Worse still, people began to confuse the serious Techno tune that Charly had set out to be with the credibility-free rip-offs. Overnight, the first new underground youth movement in more than a decade appeared to have been reduced to an infantile joke.

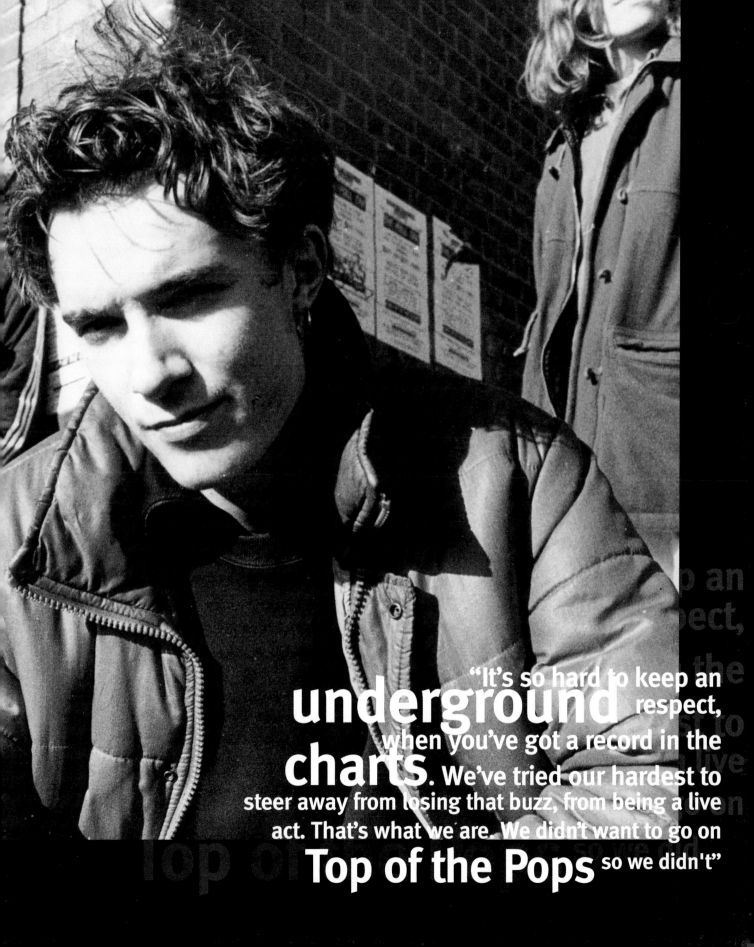

underground charts. "It's so hard to keep an respect, when you've got a record in the charts. We've tried our hardest to steer away from losing that buzz, from being a live act. That's what we are. We didn't want to go on **Top of the Pops** so we didn't"

Surprisingly, even some of the specialist dance press chose to ignore what was innovative about Charly in favour of what was mindless about its imitators. Ten months after Charly's release, with the rave scene in tatters, dance monthly Mixmag reviewed the state of play under the heading, Did Charly kill rave? On the cover of the magazine, a grimacing Liam held a gun to his head. The image proved to be prophetic. In the article, The Prodigy made a number of seriously considered, well-informed comments, both on themselves and the demise of the rave scene. The context in which those quotes were placed, however, made the band out to be enemies, rather than supporters, of the original rave ethic. The conclusion was that – yes – Charly had, albeit unintentionally, killed rave. Moreover, the band were portrayed as pathetically trying to defend their underground status. Also, bizarrely, they were mocked for being the very thing that they were most proud of – a group of good-time, up-for-it rave kids. The article remains a sore point with The Prodigy. More importantly, it was directly responsible for the band becoming incredibly mistrustful of the press. To this day, they hate doing media interviews and, when they do agree to one, usually tend to be less than forthcoming. Taken in isolation, however, Liam's comments in the Mixmag article remain a good indication of his attitude at the time. "It's so hard to keep an underground respect," he noted, "when you've got a record in the charts. We've tried our hardest to steer away from losing that buzz, from being a live act. That's what we are. We didn't want to go on Top of the Pops, so we didn't. We didn't want to go in Smash Hits and all the other stupid magazines and stuff. Any interviews we did we thought through carefully, and were in well-read and respected magazines."

On The Prodigy's commercial success, he commented: "If you're looking at it from a business point of view, we hit the scene at just the right time. We hit it at a peak. It was when all the fuckin' rave albums like Hardcore Ecstasy were out, and it established us as a band."

Finally, on contributing to rave's destruction: "Doesn't bother me, really. There's no point in thinking that, because we've had a really good time, and that's all we set out to do. Once the rave scene's died out, I'm still going to carry on. Rave is just one section of

"Nine out of ten dance tunes all sound the same. What I'm doing is to make it into some kind of mix, so it all flows through – as if you were at a rave, listening to a DJ playing. You've got the highs and lows – the piano songs are uplifting, but next to those you've got something hard"

music. I'm not just going to jump on the bandwagon, though I'll go with the flow."

The irony of The Prodigy being blamed for Charly's imitators was that it had been Liam Howlett's innovation that had made Charly so special in the first place. It was more successful than any previous rave record because Liam had not simply copied other songs, but added a brand new element. He had put not only the energy and sense of fun from the rave scene into his records, but also the experimentation.

Still a teenager and one of the youngest music-makers on the scene, Liam was, undoubtedly, among the first British musicians to cause Acid House to progress. Most notably, he introduced breakbeats – still usually associated with his former musical love, Hip-Hop – to House and Techno. He was also experimenting with the use of samples, rather than simply building an entire song around them.

"Nine out of ten dance tunes all sound the same," said the 19-year-old. "What I'm doing is to make it into some kind of mix, so it all flows through: as if you were at a rave, listening to a DJ playing. You've got the highs and lows – the piano songs are uplifting, but next to those, you've got something hard."

Even with Charly, which was, in fact, a four-track EP, Liam endeavoured to serve up some variety. "Mainly because I didn't want Charly to be seen as a novelty record," he said, "I made sure the tracks on the flip side were radically different." In particular, the hectic, upbeat Your Love, which contained vocals and piano, stood out, remaining an underground favourite even after Charly took off.

Exactly a month after Charly came out, when there were still some credible, large-scale raves around, The Prodigy played the biggest PA of their career to date, in front of 30,000 people in a tent at Perception in Cirencester.

"It means more to us to play a big rave," explained Liam, "than to chart with a single. Live, you can see the reaction for yourself, the feedback is instant."

Until then, N-Joi were undoubtedly the biggest live act on the rave circuit. The Prodigy had been one step down in popularity, along with the likes of Altern 8, Shades of Rhythm, Dream Frequency and 808 State. Understandably, Charly's success promoted the band to the top. Musically, however, they were already well ahead of most of their peers, who still tended to compose entire songs from a sample of other people's music. Now, The Prodigy's live show also began to ease ahead of the competition.

"We work our live show along the same lines as N-Joi and Shades of Rhythm, both of whom I have a great respect for," Liam told Melody Maker. "It's a shame more dance acts don't think about that side of things instead of

just aimlessly wandering about the stage. Even when I'm not actually playing, I go to a lot of raves and I'm forever hearing people moan when a PA is announced."

In fact, The Prodigy were one of the first rave acts in the country to feature both dancers and an MC on stage – a set-up that soon became common, no doubt because of their success. None of the other acts, however, could match the vibe that The Prodigy somehow managed to conjure up. Despite perceptions that Liam Howlett alone was The Prodigy, it was already obvious that the live show played an integral part in the band's success. It required a combination of both the music and the stage show to bring to life what was special about The Prodigy – to create The Prodigy experience.

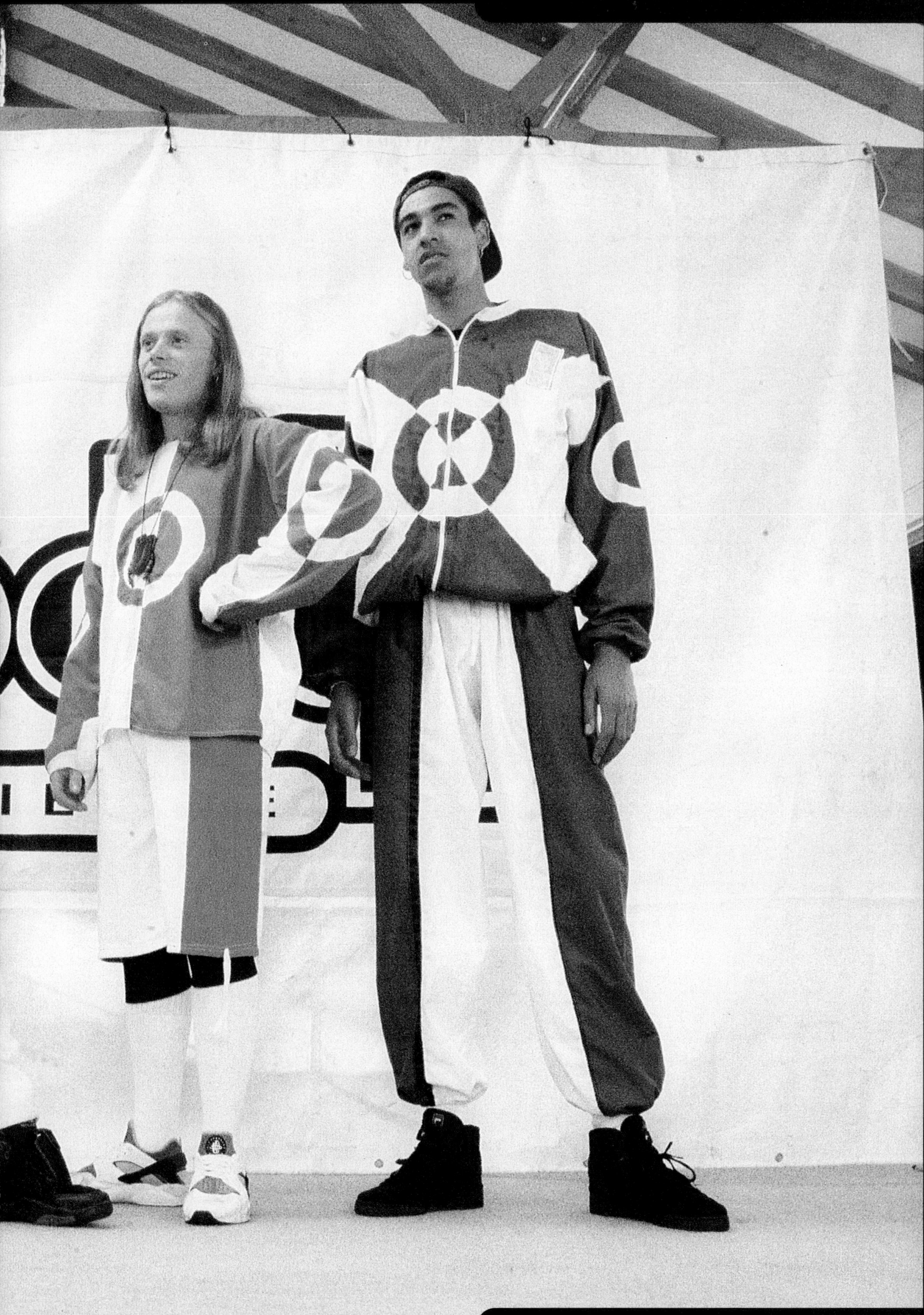

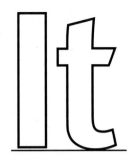

It was at a venue called The Barn in Rayne in Essex that, in the summer of 1989, 17-year-old Liam Howlett first got into rave. He had heard about the cavernous club from schoolfriends who had been regulars for months already. Liam, however, had never bothered to check The Barn out, since the few Acid House tunes he had caught on pirate radio hadn't appealed to him at all. It wasn't his type of music. It wasn't Hip-Hop.

"When I was 14 years old," recalled Liam in Melody Maker, "I used to record stuff off the radio and do mixes with the pause button on my cassette player. I've always loved doing mixes. I never liked sport or anything like that. Mixing tunes together was just what I always wanted to do."

In his early teens, Liam persuaded his dad (who had earlier forced him to take lessons in classical piano) to buy him Ska's Greatest Hits, his first ever record. At school, he introduced friends to 2-Tone bands like The Selector and The Specials. In return, one of them introduced him to melodic, American rappers such as Grandmaster Flash. Liam quickly fell for the whole Hip-Hop scene. He not only loved the mixing, scratching and heavy beats on the records, but also the visual extras, such as the dress code, graffiti artwork and flamboyant breakdancing.

One try at real mixing – on a friend's bedroom 4-track – and Liam was hooked. He took a job on a local building site to save up for two turntables, then spent hours every night practising. As soon as he felt confident enough to play in front of others, he approached a local, school-age, Hip-Hop outfit called Cut to Kill. They already had a DJ, but they took Liam on, giving him his first taste of performing in public at tiny Essex venues such as the YMCA in Chelmsford. Since he was studying for an A-level in graphic design, Liam started making flyers for the band. When he passed his exam, he took a day job on a London free magazine called Metropolitan, and continued to DJ at night. His boss at the magazine eventually heard all about Cut to Kill and, after seeing some of their gigs, proposed that he manage them. He put up £4,000 for the band to record an album.

When it was finished, however, there was no money left to release it, and a trawl round several established record companies proved fruitless.

It was at this time that Liam decided to check out The Barn. He was beginning to dislike the edgy, unfriendly vibe in many of the Hip-Hop clubs – he felt particularly uncomfortable with their attitude to what they

"I've always loved doing mixes. I never liked sport or anything like that. **Mixing tunes** together was just what I always wanted to do" – Liam

perceived as white outsiders. Future Shamen rapper Mr C was then The Barn's resident DJ, while the

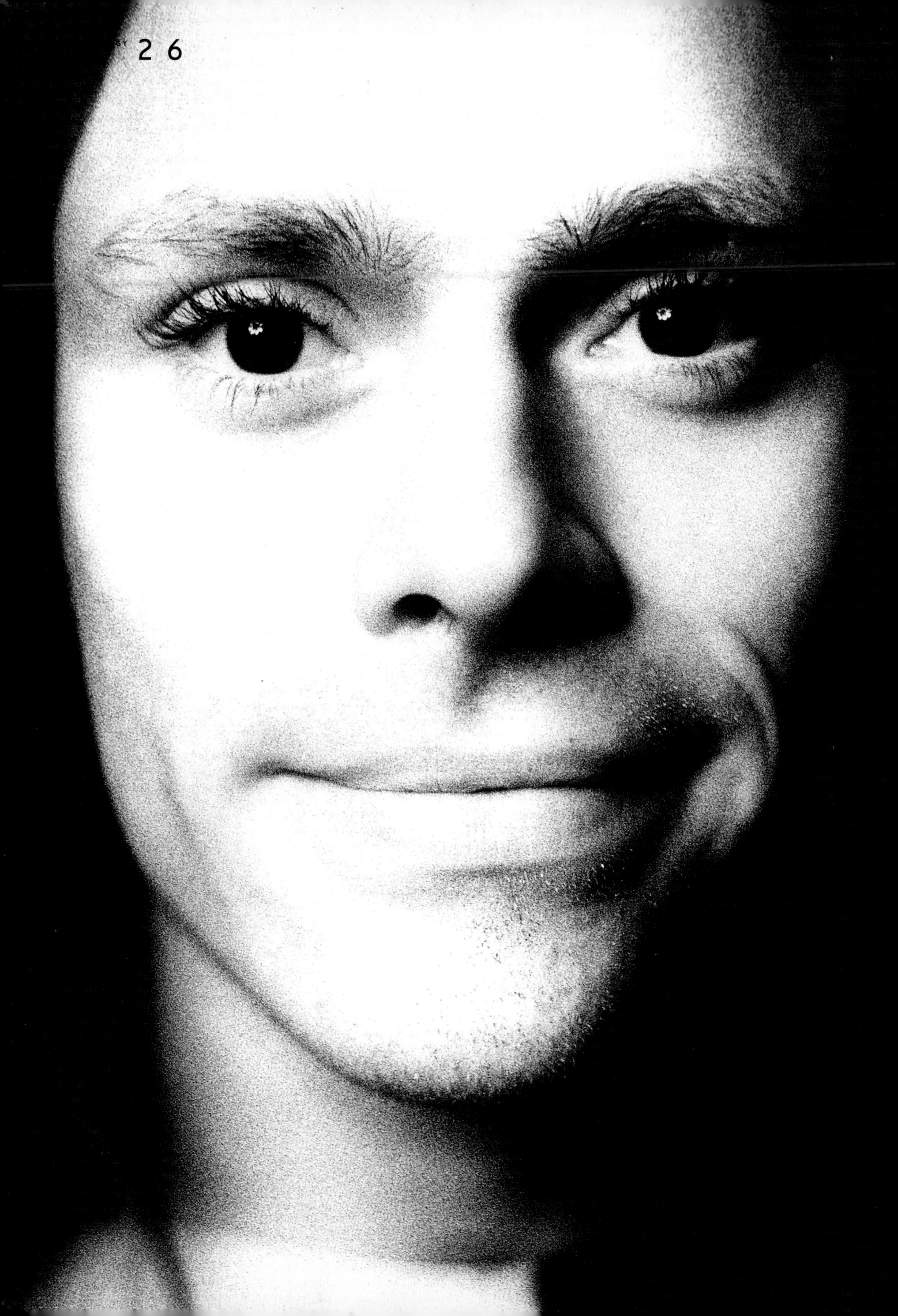

> "That first night at **The Barn** was such a stark contrast to the pretentious, exclusivist scene I was used to. I really loved the music and the whole **vibe**" – Liam

country's biggest rave acts, such as N-Joi, Shades of Rhythm and Guru Josh, regularly performed PAs there. Barely half an hour after entering the club for the first time, Liam reckons he was converted to rave. The communal, easy-going, E-drenched atmosphere inside was a pleasant shock.

"That first night at The Barn," Liam later recalled, "was such a stark contrast to the pretentious, exclusivist scene I was used to. I really loved the music and the whole vibe. I had never been into dancing that much, but here, it didn't matter. You could just smile and jump around and still enjoy yourself. You didn't have to dance properly or anything."

Liam soon split from Cut to Kill, when the rest of the band signed a short-term singles deal with an independent label on the strength of what Liam believed to be one of his own compositions – not that he minded much. He was already far more interested in writing the type of tunes that would go down well at any of the rave parties that he was now attending every weekend.

Liam spent the next year clubbing non-stop. He had a new job at a T-shirt-printing factory, and all his money went on either going out or buying records. Although he attended raves at various venues, The Barn remained his favourite. However, since it shut at 1am, the regulars tended to drive off in carloads to outdoor parties afterwards. Often, they would end up at a huge house on a nearby hillside, owned by an old hippie who didn't mind them setting up decks and strobes and sound systems out in his garden.

It was while DJing in a Transit van outside the house one night in early '91, that Liam was approached by a scruffy, long-haired raver in an Afghan coat. Liam knew his face from the local scene, but the two had never talked before. The bloke had wandered over to compliment the DJ on his set, and he introduced himself as Keith Flint.

Having left school as early as possible, unqualified for anything, Keith Flint spend his late teenage years getting through a series of dead-end jobs. He was always too interested in having a good time to worry about work. Once a smartly dressed "casual" who spent his spare time posing with his mates in trendy clubs, he decided to grow his hair, invest in a moped and start hanging out at music festivals, where he met up with a bunch of dope-smoking hippies. He got into rock bands like Led Zeppelin and Pink Floyd, and began to travel around the country.

Keith eventually jacked in whatever job it was he had at the time and headed off for eight months alone, hitchhiking through Europe and the Middle East. By the time he returned to Braintree, rave had taken over many of the local clubs. His first night out at The Barn was as unforgettable as Liam's. Keith, however, was more into just letting himself go by showing off on the dancefloor. That, to him, was probably more important than the music and most of the new mates he was meeting. He did, however, strike up one particularly important friendship – with fellow raver Leeroy Thornhill. Like Keith, Leeroy had been away from Essex when rave took off. He wasn't abroad, but was working as an electrician in Bath. Having heard about the scene through friends,

Leeroy – a big James Brown and American soul fan, who had latterly got into Electro, Hip-Hop and breakdancing – occasionally returned home at weekends to check out the clubs. He wasn't too impressed. He loved dancing and found it impossible to get a rhythm going to Acid House. Then, one night, he took Ecstasy for the first time. Suddenly, he got to grips with the fast-paced beats. Nevertheless, he retained his soulful, high-stepping style. At around 6'4", he certainly stood out from the rest of the crowd at The Barn. He was, claimed Keith, the coolest dancer there. The pair became best friends when both realised that they wanted to go out to clubs every night of the week. They became regulars at Raindance, Perception and the Astoria, as well as The Barn, and were often accompanied by a mutual friend and equally avid dancer, a girl called Sharky.

It was after returning from a night out at Raindance that Keith eventually listened to the tape that Liam had made up for him, following their initial meeting at the after-Barn party. Keith had enjoyed Liam's set so much that he asked him for a cassette of something similar. Liam mixed up a few tunes on one side of the tape, then recorded a couple of his own compositions on the B-side, just to find out what Keith thought of them. Keith and Leeroy listened to the tape together. The first side was great – but the second side was even better. Both were so taken by Liam's songs that they immediately started to dance around Keith's house, working out different routines to perform to each track. On the outside of the tape, observed Keith, was scribbled the name The Prodigy – referring to the keyboard model, Moog Prodigy, on which the songs had been created. Keith took it to be Liam's moniker.

That weekend, Keith and Leeroy approached Liam at The Barn and suggested that they get a dance act going with the three of them, plus their dancer friend Sharky. Liam liked the idea, but also wanted to find an MC to front the band. It was a friend of Keith's called Ziggy who suggested Maxim Reality. Ziggy had a lot of contacts on the dance scene. He booked The Prodigy their first gig at The Labyrinth in Dalston, and so they decided to take him on as their manager. Ziggy had seen Maxim Reality (real name Keith Palmer) MC-ing in his home town of Peterborough, where he was well known on the local reggae circuit.

Maxim had always been into writing poetry and verse, and had learnt to MC from his older brother, Starkey Ban Tan. He liked Hip-Hop and breakdancing, but was most interested in Reggae. While doing a YTS in electronic maintenance, Maxim teamed up with an experienced musician from Nottingham, who called himself Sheik Yan Groove. Together, they fused Reggae, Hip-Hop and world percussion, as Maxim discovered a host of new influences such as jazz, blues and George Clinton's P-Funk collective. After a couple of years spent trying in vain to attract attention from record companies, Maxim took three months off, then moved to London. Although he soon got involved in the capital's underground Reggae scene, he was still searching for a proper break into the industry. When Ziggy invited him to front a brand new rave band at their debut gig, Maxim wasn't sure. He decided, however, that it was too good an opportunity to miss.

The Prodigy's first PA, at the Labyrinth in a rather dodgy area of northeast London, marked only the second time a band had ever performed at the venue. The last band, according to the manager, had been bottled off. The Prodigy were so nervous that they turned up 10 hours before they were due on stage. They had simply to set up, calm themselves down and change into the outfits they had made the previous week. At that time, all the rave acts wore costumes, so they had sewed together five green and white suits, each with a circular pattern across the chest. Keith, Leeroy and Sharky had also memorised a number of dance routines to perform to Liam's songs.

Several hours later, Maxim

arrived. It was the first time any of the others had met him. He read through the set list of eight songs. He still wasn't sure about this. He had been to a couple of raves before and never really enjoyed himself. As for the rest of the band, they simply hoped that at least some of the numerous clubbing mates they had invited would turn up. In the end, about 250 people were present to witness The Prodigy live for the first time.

Two songs into the set, and even Maxim was starting to enjoy the gig. It was so good, in fact, that the club's owner invited the band back to play the following Saturday, when there would be at least 1000 people there. They accepted straight away. There was, however, one fairly serious problem: Liam liked Maxim and sensed from his debut, highly improvised performance that he had something special. His very lyrical Reggae style, however, wasn't at all right for a rave act. Liam told Maxim that if he could reduce his raps to a series of simple one-liners, preferably related to the rave spirit, he would like him to become a permanent member of The Prodigy. Maxim not only knew what he meant, but felt he could offer something more than the regular rave MCs. That sorted, The Prodigy was fixed as a five-piece, and regular club PAs started to come their way.

It was just before Christmas 1990 that Liam called the band together for a special announcement: he had a record deal. They were shocked. All four had joined the band simply for fun. Their biggest ambition had been to play at an outdoor event such as Raindance. For almost a year, however, Liam had been writing dozens of rave tunes and laying down demos, usually in the early hours of the morning, after a mad night out. He had sent a 10-track cassette of his work off to two record labels to gauge their reaction. The second – recently formed dance specialists XL, a subsidiary of Beggars Banquet – had got in touch immediately. Liam travelled to London to see XL's two directors, Tim Palmer and Nick Halkes. The pair liked not only the innovative elements they could hear in Liam's roughly recorded demo, but also the 18-year-old's underground attitude. Even more importantly, they felt that he had the vision to make his music progress beyond rave. Similarly, Liam liked XL, especially when he discovered that Tim Palmer's mother was the old lady who had regularly sold him underground techno imports at London's Groove Record shop.

At that time, Liam was taking his musical influences not only from the white-label rave records he heard out at night, but also from established artists such as Renegade Soundwave, Meat Beat Manifesto and DJ Joel Beltram. Significantly, he was recording his material on a Roland W30, as opposed to the rave standard Ataris. This equipment gave Liam's tunes the unusually rough, ropy, almost nasty edge that was soon to become The Prodigy's trademark.

In February 1991, The Prodigy released their first single, a 4-track EP titled What Evil Lurks. All of the tracks were lifted from Liam's original demo: Android, Everybody In The Place, We're Gonna Rock and Evil Lurks, the latter stealing a sample – "What evil lurks in the heart of men" – from The Shadow radio series of the 1940s.

With a product in the shops, The Prodigy were booked to play endless PAs. They averaged between three and six gigs a week, played their first foreign date (in Italy), and were sometimes seen by up to 5,000 people a night. Even when the band wasn't booked for a major event, the DJ would inevitably play at least one track from their EP. A rhythmic burst of dark backbeats, eerie synth sounds and deep bass, What Evil Lurks peaked at No. 31 in the dance charts, finally sold a respectable 7,000 copies, and earned the band their first-ever review.

"Why The Prodigy?" asked Mixmag Update of the EP. "Because creator Liam Howlett is but 19 years old. I don't think I've ever been to Essex, but the exploits of Mark Ryder, N-Joi, D-Zone and now Mr. Howlett paint a vivid picture of a raver-filled country, a natural extension of the East End House scene. That end of the Central Line likes its music hard, and this collection of breakbeat-driven Techno will not disappoint. Crunchy stuff indeed (and, er, "Respect to the Braintree posse")."

With the exception of Liam – who had long since decided that his future lay in music – The Prodigy had never regarded this band as much more than a hobby. Suddenly, it was serious. This was time to either get professional or get out. Only Sharky opted to leave. Now an all-male four-piece, The Prodigy got down to band business properly for the first time. Keith and Leeroy agreed never to take Ecstasy again before going on stage. Buzzing from Liam's music alone, they could be sure to turn in an inspired performance every night. Moreover, if they wanted to improve, they would have to rehearse. The band's very first practice session, however, was hopeless. Oddly, Leeroy, Keith and Maxim all felt incredibly awkward and embarrassed about recreating their stage show in Liam's parents' house. It was unreal, phoney somehow. Half an hour later, The Prodigy had decided never to rehearse again.

All this time, the rave scene was growing in popularity almost as quickly as The Prodigy. While Keith and Leeroy achieved an early ambition when the band played at Raindance, many of the original venues (including The Barn) had already closed down. Meanwhile, dozens of new clubs, largely run by profit-hungry promoters, were opening up almost every week. It was at a night called Telepathy in northeast London, recalls Keith, that out of the blue, on stage, Liam unleashed an astonishing hardcore track on both the audience and his fellow band members for the first time. The tune was called Charly – and it was just about to detonate rave.

The tune was called **Charly** – and it was just about to detonate **rave**

chapter three

Charly's unexpected crossover success brought with it a number of changes within The Prodigy. The band gave up their day jobs, took on their own tour crew and technicians and decided to recruit a professional manager. They approached Mike Champion, then co-manager of N-Joi. Already a fan of The Prodigy's live show, Champion needed only to meet the band to be persuaded to leave N-Joi in the hands of his partner. The effect of Champion's experience was immediate. Liam's deal with XL was quickly – and very favourably – renegotiated. Their now non-stop PAs were meticulously organised, and their earnings ploughed back into the band, while various lines of merchandising, designed largely by Liam, went into production.

In late 91, The Prodigy set off to Germany for their first foreign tour, before flying to New York to play a small gig at the Limelight Club and shooting the video for the follow-up to Charly, Everybody in the Place, a remix of a track from the What Evil Lurks EP. An endearingly simple, haphazardly compiled montage of clips of The Prodigy dancing awkwardly on street corners, getting in and out of cabs and pestering resident New Yorkers, the video was a light-hearted contrast to the song itself. Everybody in the Place was, in fact, another 4-track EP, which also featured the songs Crazy Man, Rip up the Sound System and G Force, the latter the first tune to be written on Liam's new U220 Roland sound module. "There's probably a lot of people," noted Echoes magazine in their review of the EP, "who, as Liam Howlett feared, now see The Prodigy as a one-hit wonder/novelty. The follow-up had to be a no-holds-barred killer to continue the momentum from their scorching PAs. This should do the trick. The main cut is a propulsive breakbeat raver that sounds like Primal Scream's Come Together speeded up. The other tracks continue the buzz – every sound is geared up to maintaining maximum mass mayhem."

"We don't see ourselves as **stars**. Maybe that's one reason why we appeal: because we look like people in the crowd who have jumped up on **stage**"

Incredibly for such a hardcore release, Everybody in the Place went one better than Charly.

"People into **hardcore** like doing **Es** and getting a really good **vibe** going. The club scene is more **sophisticated.** It's all designer beers and trying to pull birds. There's not that heavy buzz of spiritual togetherness that you get at a **rave**"

doing **ES** and getting
lub scene is more
designer be and
t heavy bu spiritual
vo

The **Prodigy** are more than just a **rave** act.
We're much more musical

Kept off the top spot only by a reissue of Queen's Bohemian Rhapsody, it peaked at No. 2 in the national charts, despite the band's persistent refusal to appear on TV shows such as Top of the Pops.

"Why should we go on telly so some pompous wanker can say, 'Oh, I really liked the words to that one?' " pointed out Liam. "We don't see ourselves as stars. Maybe that's one reason why we appeal: because we look like people in the crowd who have jumped up on stage."

The rave roots that were still very much present in The Prodigy's records, however, did incite criticism from a section of the dance community who believed that serious Techno bands should be distancing themselves from the now commercially successful rave scene. Of the EP, Mixmag commented: "This isn't Techno, because the real stuff is cleverly put together. It's not underground unless you take my advice and bury it. It's definitely not sophisticated – this is a record made for children, by children. There is no love of music involved at all, just a 'let's knock it out' attitude that sucks. This is most definitely a throwaway record."

Liam retaliated by denouncing the softer, more melodic Progressive House that many of the magazines, in particular, were wishing would replace rave.

"I hope people don't go over to that stuff," he told Melody Maker. "I don't like it. It's for people who can't keep up with the rave scene. It's totally different. People into hardcore like doing Es and getting a really good vibe going. The club scene is more sophisticated. It's all designer beers and trying to pull birds. There's not that heavy buzz of spiritual togetherness that you get at a rave."

The Prodigy did not release a record for a further nine months, although Liam did receive his first remix commissions, first for Dream Frequency, then for The Art of Noise. In accepting the latter, he joined the likes of Carl Cox, 808 State and Youth in reworking tracks for the defunct band's Fon Mixes album. Liam's offering, however, was barely related to the original. A remix request from Take That was turned down forthright.

In the wake of their singles success, The Prodigy spent the following months touring the UK and Europe, returning to the States in early 92 to play a handful of low-key dates in major cities such as L.A., New York and Miami. It was while there that they signed a US record deal with Electra (Altern 8 had just negotiated a similar contract), as well as an Australian deal with Sony.

In September 92, with their debut album, Experience, about to be released, The Prodigy put out the single Fire for just one week (even the promo video, shot in Wales, was abandoned). Boasting a sample nabbed – somewhat ironically – from a novelty 1960s hit of the same name, by a band called The Crazy World of Arthur Brown, Fire featured a deep, dubby bassline, snatches of piano and recognisable Reggae influences. It reached No. 11 in the national charts (topping the dance charts like every Prodigy release to date), while the B-side, the scary jungle tune Horns of Jericho, even found favour with many of the élitist, underground DJs.

"Despite The Prodigy's unfortunate, but inevitable, commercial success with any track they lay their name to," commented Mixmag Update, "I can safely say that Fire is a defiant monster. A touch harder than their normal offerings, making it that bit better than previous releases. The A-side has a natty little synth line and some deep, deep bass, but the much stronger track is Horns of Jericho. This is an excellent piece of serious hardcore breakbeat, drop-dead dinky little killer riff, heavy Jungle feel, and not recommended to anyone who is faint-hearted. If there were only a thousand whites [white labels] of this, ALL the

"**Experience** is a kick in the teeth for all those **sad people** who thought that **Techno** was just a **one-dimensional**, narcotic flash-in-the-pan"

scene. A brutal, uncompromising frenzy of hyperspeed BPMs, accelerated breakbeats and screamed slogans to attract new converts to techno, it was still a milestone for alternative dance music. In 1992, Acid House-inspired singles could often claim up to half the Top 20 national-chart placings. The only hard dance albums that sold well, however, were Various Artists compilations of recent hits. Altern 8 had attained moderate success with their patchwork LP, but Experience was undoubtedly the first original, largely instrumental Techno record to prove that hardcore dance acts had the potential to be viable album artists. In fact, neither the band nor XL had even considered the prospect of a Prodigy LP until fairly recently. Liam was happy to be signed only to a singles deal. Then he realised that to release all the material he had on just this format would not only take months, but would also hinder any progression of The Prodigy.

"I was going to make the LP a rave concept album at first," confessed Liam to Melody Maker. "Then I changed my mind, because I think The Prodigy are more than just a rave act. We're much more musical. That's why I'd like to do something leftfield in the future – a real Pink Floyd-type ambient album, maybe a concept LP about the sun, or something. First though, I need to establish The Prodigy more solidly."

Single-handedly written, recorded, engineered and

underground crew would go apeshit to get hold of one, due to its quality. Maybe it's worth trying once, for the respect."

Later that month came Experience, one of the first – and easily the most eagerly awaited – full-length albums to emerge from the rave produced by Liam, and pressed over two vinyl LPs for a greater depth of sound, Experience (the title nicked from a posthumous 70s Hendrix album) entered the UK charts at No. 12, eventually selling around 200,000 copies. All of the band's singles so far (not to mention two future releases) appeared in vastly remixed form: Charly, most notably, not only took on a Jungle tinge, but also had its cartoon sample cut to barely one second.

"Experience is a kick in the teeth for all those sad people who thought that Techno was just a one-dimensional, narcotic flash-in-the-pan," said music monthly Select, who awarded the album five out of five. "On the basis that albums last where hit singles fade into the ether, this one should have kids knocking back Lucozade well into the next century."

Significantly, one track stood out from all the others. A relatively tranquil, almost ambient, distinctly Floydian excursion, Weather Experience, claimed Liam, was included to show that his writing need not necessarily revolve around breakbeat structures. He was, he said, hoping to compose film scores at some time in the future.

Whether by coincidence or design, Experience marked the final breath of rave's drawn-out, undignified demise. Unscrupulous promoters had long-since muscled in on large-scale events. Now, it was almost as hard to find a decent rave tune as it was to buy pure MDMA.

"Nearly all white labels are now shit," noted Liam. "Nobody's being creative anymore. Everyone just uses the same samples. Technology has let the scene down really. It's too easy to knock up a tune for £500."

The communal, feelgood factor had definitely disappeared, and even the bands were bitching about each other. Liam, in Melody Maker, on fellow dance innovators Shut Up and Dance: "Fuck them. They slagged us off and said that we were ripping them off because they were jealous of our success. Then I saw them miming on the Hitman and Her. Some of the music is quite good, but I think they're pathetic, really."

In November 92, The Prodigy headed out on the 23-date British tour to promote Experience. They took with them a mammoth sound system, a customised PA flown in specially from the States and a lighting rig with heliographic lasers and computer animation. Most importantly, though, they played traditional rock and indie venues such as The Barrowlands in Glasgow and Aston Villa Leisure Centre, rather than sticking to the established rave circuit. Financially, that proved to be a disaster. For starters, dance promoters had no idea how to advertise conventionally staged concerts. Furthermore, dance fans had grown out of the idea of going to gigs. It was boring, they assumed, to just stand and watch a band: live performances midway through an actual event were what they wanted. Consequently, The Prodigy often found themselves playing to half-capacity crowds.

To coincide with the tour, the fourth single from Experience, Out of Space, was released. An eerie Ragga tune, featuring a sampled Max Romeo phrase from Chase the Devil, Out of Space made the Top 3 of the national chart, undoubtedly aided by its bizarre, hilarious video. Filmed outside what looks like a farmhouse, Keith dresses up as a demented raver, in an outfit that includes white overalls, pink, rubber kitchen gloves and a tub of Vicks Vapour Rub taped to the nose of his face mask. Perhaps unsurprisingly, Altern 8 (whose outfits, while more serious, were not entirely dissimilar) thought that The Prodigy were trying to take the piss. In their next video, Altern 8 would pretend to be The Prodigy.

That

Christmas was spent in Australia, on a brief, five-date tour with legendary DJ Paul Oakenfold. It proved, however, to be an ill-advised pairing. Oakenfold's melodic, slow-paced sets jarred with The Prodigy's frantic live performances. Neither act was prepared to compromise and the crowds were left confused. At one of the gigs, a New Year's Eve party, Oakenfold exasperated the situation by dropping snatches of what the band believed to be The Smarties' Sesame's Treet. Already exhausted, The Prodigy flew directly from Australia to the States, where they were scheduled to play 28 concerts in one month, on a bill with Moby, as well as film a video for their forthcoming single. It proved to be the low point of the band's career. Not only had they to travel long distances on a shared tour bus – which had formerly belonged to The Eagles and had Hotel California emblazoned down both sides – but the conditions in both the venues and the hotels were frequently appalling. Worse still, many of the promoters refused to pay up after the shows. Demoralised, in debt and ill from overwork, The Prodigy headed back to Britain.

> "Everyone just uses the same samples. **Technology** has let the scene **down** really. It's too easy to knock up a **tune** for £500"

It

was March 93 and Wind It Up, the fifth Experience single, described by Mixmag Update as "2-Tone Ragga raving", had just entered the UK Top Three. Liam, however, hated the thought of putting out another track from the album. For one thing, it looked like a Michael Jackson-style squeeze on the fans. For another, it was, by now, a dated track. It reinforced The Prodigy's association with the very scene from which they were desperately trying to distance themselves. Moreover, although he had secretly been in a studio for months, in Liam's mind, The Prodigy's sound was currently undergoing an enormous change.

"Around that time", commented Liam later, "we were looking to change the music, to get away from the breakbeat and do something a bit more Techno. We were listening to all these tunes from abroad, which we had heard on tour. It was labels like Sub Base and Movin' Shadow that remained the true underground sound of London, because they didn't get the chance to travel round. It we had been stuck at home and hadn't experienced different sounds from all over the world, we'd probably have continued to do breakbeat stuff, too."

The band's travels, however, were about to alter the sound of The Prodigy beyond recognition. Their recent trip to the States, in particular, was to prove a major influence. Early 93 saw Liam replace his all-time favourite album, the Ultramagnetic MCs' late 80s Hip-Hop classic Critical Beatdown, with an unlikely rival – Nirvana's grunge epic Nevermind.

"We were looking to **change** the **music**, to get away from the **breakbeat** and do something a bit more **Techno**. We were listening to all these tunes from abroad, which we had heard on **tour**"

"We were looking to cha away from the break bit more Techno tunes from abroad, which

nge the music, to get

beat and do something a

We were listening to all these

e had heard on tour"

chapter four

Frustrated

at having had to release a year-old track that he felt no longer represented The Prodigy as a brand new single, Liam spent the months leading up to the summer of 93 locked in his home studio, determined to write some radically different, more sophisticated material. The result, the single One Love, was in fact so unlike any previous Prodigy release that nobody even knew it had come from Howlett. Originally put out in two versions as a cheaply packaged white label, One Love – credited only to Earthbound, the name of Liam's own studio – allowed The Prodigy to gauge the underground's true reaction to the record. This way, the response of DJs and dance journalists would be based solely on the musical merit of One Love, and would not be influenced by opinions on The Prodigy themselves. A percussion-driven,

hardcore House track, overlaid with sparse, Arabic wailing, One Love earned not only favourable reviews, but also went down well with even the élitist DJs and club crowds. Three months later, in October, the single came out as a proper Prodigy release. It was backed by another new track, the slightly harder Rhythm of Life, and reached No. 8 in the national charts. Of the record, Mixmag Update said, "Essentially a monster, bass-heavy House tune with The Prodigy's trademark manic element, this definitely rocks, and not just for the hardcore followers. The title track is tough but accessible and should get play from a good range of DJs, while Rhythm of Life is German-influenced Techno that thumps with grace. It's a change of style, then. The Prodigy leap forward."

"Forget the **authorities**. You can't stop us. We're gonna keep the **dance** scene strong even if the **world** isn't" – Liam

"I don't wish to be seen as one of those **Techno** bods, either: I haven't innovated as much as they have. Someone like **Derrick May** has worked within the Techno sound, and never moved away from that. I just want respect for making **hard** dance music" – Liam

Techno

nose **Techno**

much as they have.
y has worked within the
ay from that. I just want
ce music" – Liam

"Oh yeah, five stars. A month later, it's in the fuckin' charts. **So what?** That wasn't why we made it. We are all of us just in The Prodigy for the **buzz"**

"I write for myself and the rest of the band – with the fans in mind"

Not everyone, however, embraced The Prodigy's new direction. "One Love lacks the maverick, individual quality that distinguished tracks like Everybody in the Place," remarked one reviewer. "This is unlikely to repeat the band's normal, routine chart success. It's a jungle out there, but this time, The Prodigy can't see the wood for the trees."

Moreover, many of the DJs who had played the original Earthbound release now shunned the single, deeming it too commercial. Not for the first time, The Prodigy found themselves at odds with the very scene they were supposed to represent. By now, though, it was obvious that the dance underground itself was undergoing big changes. The mainstream success of some of the scene's least compromising, most innovative artists meant that the original definition of underground music had become obsolete. What was once a byword for hard, often experimental, alternative dance music, now applied only to records that would not, or could not, enter the charts. Strictly limited edition releases, imports and singles so extreme that they would appeal only to a minority audience could be called underground: anything by The Prodigy was simply too popular to qualify.

Liam, understandably, stuck to the early definition of underground. To him, it meant staying true to the spirit of Acid House by refusing to compromise any aspect of the band in order to sell more records. Consequently, Liam continued to refer to The Prodigy as an underground act. He also began to look to fans of the band, rather than fickle industry insiders, to confirm the integrity of the music.

"You've got to think about the people you're writing the tunes for," he concluded at the time. "I write for myself and the rest of the band – with the fans in mind. That's why we have to gradually ease new styles in. I was aware that, because One Love had less breakbeats, it could have lost us a lot of our original following. At that point, though, the whole scene was splitting up into various categories, with one set of DJs going one way and others going elsewhere, and I didn't want to get involved in the internal politics. It would have been too limiting."

Liam also spoke out against the élite underground that refused to acknowledge The Prodigy.

"When One Love was out as Earthbound on a white label," he told Select, "all those fuckers played it. They were going, 'Oh yeah, five stars'. A month later, it's in the fuckin' charts. So what? That wasn't why we made it. We are all of us just in The Prodigy for the buzz.

"I don't wish to be seen as one of those techno bods, either: I haven't innovated as much as they have. Someone like Derrick May has worked within the techno sound, and never moved away from that. I just want respect for making hard dance music. The techno royalty thing is destructive, anyway. Look at the Aphex Twin – I like a lot of his stuff, but there's so much hype in the papers that when you go and see him, you're bound to be disappointed."

Liam,

however, hardly had to worry how the hardcore dance community perceived The Prodigy. The band's continued crossover success, combined with the new range of musical influences displayed on One Love, proved that their appeal was much more widespread – as did the remix work Liam was being offered. First, he turned indie band Jesus Jones into a brutal

Techno outfit; then he struck terror into Belgian band Front 242's Religion single. In turn, several of the European industrial bands were making their mark on The Prodigy. The intensity and energy of their sound appealed to Liam's hardcore roots. Nevertheless, he wanted to forge his own form of electronic music, which took its cue not only from Techno, but any number of other styles.

"I still love the London breakbeat scene," Liam told Select, "but you have to have an open mind to all music. The Prodigy are just a hard dance band, rather than Techno or Jungle or hardcore. We never even saw ourselves as leaders of the rave scene. In the end, we weren't the ones in the parties and the clubs every week. It was down to the DJs whether rave lived or died, not us. But it wasn't a case of us sitting down and saying, 'Right, we have to change.' It was because we travelled and experienced so many different styles of music – probably a lot more than other bands in our musical area." In fact, much to the surprise of original Prodigy followers, Liam's new musical discoveries appeared to have little in common with the background of the band. Suddenly, he was citing Senser, the Beastie Boys, Pop Will Eat Itself, Rage Against the Machine and the Red Hot Chili Peppers as his favourite acts of the year.

"The Chili Peppers are the bollocks," he told NME. "Live, they are the best band I've ever seen. The fuckin' energy up there on stage is like nothing else. And they're not a particularly hardcore guitar band, it's just good music. That's what I want us to be – a Chili Peppers for the dance scene."

With

One Love in the charts, The Prodigy set off on yet another period of touring. In the second half of 93, they played more than 60 shows in the UK, Ireland, Japan and across Europe, where their fan base was significantly boosted by MTV's decision to place One Love on heavy rotation. It was the first Prodigy video the station had ever backed. A stunning, computer-generated mix of high-tech graphics, Aztec-style artwork and snatches of the band, scaled down to resemble dancing dolls, the One Love promo was, like the track itself, a huge progression from anything The Prodigy had previously produced. It was more professional, more sophisticated and much more expensive. The image overhaul was deliberate. The band changed their style to suit both their new sound and the wider audience they were attracting. They abandoned their matching stage outfits ("We no longer fancied looking like The Stylistics," commented Liam) in favour of a far cooler skate-punk look, while all the band – bar Keith – had their hair cropped short.

It

was with the release of One Love that The Prodigy also made their first statement on the newly introduced Criminal Justice Bill. In an attempt to clamp down on the hundreds of raves and massive outdoor parties now taking place every weekend, the British Government had introduced laws to control the sound level of certain types of music.

"Repetitive beats at high volume that trance the mind," quoted Liam angrily, shortly after The Prodigy had been forced to cut short one gig after a neighbouring farmer complained about the noise. It wasn't the first time they had fallen foul of the new law.

"If this album had been the same as the first, all fast breakbeat hardcore, I would have really worried about burning out from a lack of scope"

"We played at a night called Rezerection in Scotland," explained Liam. "It was in a fuckin' airport, with planes taking off all the time, and they still took all the bass out of our set. It was pathetic. The legal limit for outdoor events is 96 decibels. You can shout louder than that." In fact, 12,000 people were present to witness The Prodigy walking off stage, midway through a show, for the very first time. The volume had been turned down so low that the planes were drowning out their set. Subsequently, the following statement was released to the press and also reprinted on some of the One Love record sleeves: "Forget the authorities. You can't stop us. We're gonna keep the dance scene strong even if the world isn't. This is your day and no one can take it away from you. The dance scene is too strong to disappear."

At the start of 94, The Prodigy took a break from touring to allow Liam into the studio to begin work on a second album. It was the first time he had ever had to write a batch of songs over a limited period. Experience was essentially a collection of singles, written, recorded and reworked over almost two years, and tried out frequently in front of massive audiences. Now, with only one track in the bag, Liam was due to deliver a brand new album by July. He was determined not only to continue the musical progression of One Love, but also to retain the buzz and energy he had first captured from the rave scene.

"I didn't really care if other people liked the album or not," noted Liam later. "Introducing other styles was going to open up another life for the band, and that's what I wanted most from the record. It was also essential for me not to feel that being in The Prodigy was tying me to one type of music. If this album had been the same as the first, all fast breakbeat hardcore, I would have really worried about burning out from a lack of scope. All the new music that I was hearing was giving me so much more range."

Nevertheless, forging a new direction for The Prodigy proved not to be as easy as Liam had hoped. Having laid down a couple of experimental backing tracks, he simply couldn't envisage a single sound that would incorporate all of the ideas he had in his head.

"When I write," he explained, "I am inspired by a feeling or an environment, rather than a specific event. Then I try to recreate the same atmosphere within the song. I'm attempting to set exactly the same scene for other people. That's why I have to get a certain buzz or tingle about every sound or sample or riff to know that it's right. If it has an effect on me, then I know it's working. For me, the object of

"We played at a night called **Rezerection** in Scotland. It was in a fuckin' airport. It was **pathetic...** The legal limit for outdoor events is **96 decibels.** You can **shout louder** than that" – Liam

"I was just lookin'
after it... it woz on a fuckin'
shelf... yoscan't arrest me for
that" – Liam

Most people take ambient music to mean nice floaty sounds like The Orb or Aphex Twin. I think of ambient as music that creates an atmosphere, which is exactly what I try to do. I see myself as an ambient artist. When I write, I get pictures in my head and just come up with suitable music to accompany the scene. I guess it's the same as writing a soundtrack – and Flash Gordon is, without doubt, the ultimate soundtrack album

writing music is to touch an emotion, and that's what I wanted every track on the album to do."

Becoming increasingly confused by his own wealth of ideas, Liam decided to take a month off to forget about trying to write, and then come back to the album fresh. He took up snowboarding and discovered that it gave him almost as big a buzz as being in a band. He then went on holiday and, oddly, became fascinated with the terminally unhip Prog Rock records of the 1970s. Already a Pink Floyd fan, he also got into Deep Purple and – most importantly, he reckons – Queen's Flash Gordon soundtrack album.

"I think it's an amazing LP," he confessed. "I listened to it so many times and it inspired me so much. The attention to detail in every track is incredible. To me, that's a real ambient album. Most people take ambient music to mean nice floaty sounds like The Orb or Aphex Twin. I think of ambient as music that creates an atmosphere, which is exactly what I try to do. I see myself as an ambient artist. When I write, I get pictures in my head and just come up with suitable music to accompany the scene. I guess it's the same as writing a soundtrack – and Flash Gordon is, without doubt, the ultimate soundtrack album."

With this new method of writing now clear in his mind, Liam returned to the studio and began work immediately. The first track down was Break and Enter, a song with manic beats that harked back to Charly's chaotic rhythm section.

"Break and Enter suggests a moral ambiguity at the heart of The Prodigy's ethos," said NME. "Its theme of daylight robbery could be a metaphor for subverting the system, or could just be a wanton celebration of criminality – the actual crushing dance track offers no clues."

Liam was determined to make the next track completely different. He wrote future single Voodoo People based entirely on live segments of music, because he wanted to create at least one song with no synths. Then, deciding to speak out for the second time against the increasingly draconian Criminal Justice Bill, he accepted an invitation to collaborate with indie band Pop Will Eat Itself.

"Although I had been listening to a lot of guitar music since around the time of One Love," admitted Liam, "I had never actually considered incorporating guitars into my songs. When Pop Will Eat Itself sent me their track, I chopped it up and got Their Law, based only on parts of the main riff. The result had a very street, skateboard feel. There's surf guitars, Hip-Hop, real drums and very heavy beats all in there. I loved that song because it had a proper band sound." Of the record, NME concluded: "If it's obvious, screaming hit singles you're after, you could do a lot worse than soon-to be-released anthem, Their Law, wherein Liam Howlett meets Pop Will Eat

Itself in a clash of wills, a battle between deep, electronic bass and howling, riff-tastic guitars that puts the Criminal Justice Bill into perspective."

Soon, the concept of the album had fallen into place. Half the core ideas were an extension of Experience, half were brand new. Notably, however, it was Liam's desire to experiment with unorthodox song structures that finally cemented The Prodigy sound.

"I've got really into weird arrangements and chord progressions," he explained. "I like to do the unexpected and I guess that's where my technical training on the piano is useful. It allows me to come up with melodies very quickly from only a simple bassline."

On some of the new tracks, Liam brought in former N-Joi producer Neil McClellan to assist. McClellan later claimed that he was amazed by not only the speed at which Liam completed tracks, but also his unique writing technique. "He doesn't even have a vast knowledge of the gear he is using," commented McClellan. "Not that it's state-of-the-art stuff. A Roland W30 is something you buy as your first piece of gear – real low-tech – but that makes absolutely no difference.

"Liam plays everything in manually, rather than looping sections all the time. It's incredible to watch. He also starts each new track differently. Sometimes, he'll tune all the keyboards down to a certain sample, so that none of the equipment is really in the key it says it is. We got other sounds by trying all sorts of mad things. For example, we put a speaker underneath a grand piano playing a 303 bassline, taped up all the piano strings, then put an effects box in there as well. Another time, we put a brick on the piano's sustain pedal, so that all the strings were just above the hammer, then we fed the effects unit through there again. As a recording process, it was completely unique. No matter how experimental a lot of music may appear to be at first, somewhere along the line, an orthodoxy will develop, and a traditional structure or methodology that you can recognise is sure to creep in. That never happened with Liam."

Without doubt, the most surprising track that came out of those sessions was Poison. At just 104 BPM, it was the slowest track Liam had written since his Hip-Hop beginnings. "That song could have lost us a lot of fans because it's so laid back," observed Liam. "But I wanted to prove that hard sounds did not necessarily involve fast speeds. I also wanted to make more use of Maxim. He actually tried out a few vocal ideas at first that didn't quite work. Then he came back with the Poison lyric. That style is unique to him: it's not Rap or Reggae or rave. I loved the drug ambiguities in it, too. His input gave me the buzz to get that track totally right. Poison became a key element of the album and the musical direction I was going in, because it was completely different to anything on Experience."

At the end of the album was a three-song concept piece about the drugs scene called The Narcotic Suite.

"Tacky drug references aside," said Select, "The Narcotic Suite transports a single musical theme into three dancefloor idioms: zoned-out Santana-funk on 3 Kilos, spectral Trance on Skylined and manic Acid on Claustrophobic Sting. But even this ambitious conceit is overshadowed by the breathtaking Speedway, a theme piece where roaring motorbikes are joined by layer upon layer of fractious Acid patterns, building up to a pitch of immense tension."

"All of those tracks," explained Liam later, "came from images in my head. For 3 Kilos, I pictured a load of laid back people lying around a smoky room; Skylined had an uplifting, rush feel to it; and Claustrophobic Sting was a paranoid, depths-of-hell track, probably the most forbidding music I've ever written. Speedway was also very visual. It was programmed to sound as though these bikes were flying out at you."

Ironically, it was one of the very few new tracks not written in this way that was chosen as the next single to be taken from the album. No Good (Start the Dance) was simply a hard club song, rather than a soundtrack to a visual image. Nevertheless, it was to prove yet another, genre-defying, monster hit for The Prodigy.

chapter five

Prior

to its release, The Prodigy had been playing No Good (Start the Dance) – their eighth single and seventh consecutive hit – for over six months at regular gigs and PAs. Consequently, although it was a definite move away from straightforward breakbeats to a more complex fusion of styles, the song was not nearly as big a musical step on from Experience as the more recent material Liam had been writing. In addition, it seemed to lack the obvious Prodigy hook that had, by now, become the band's trademark. Having opted against slowing the track from 150 to 130 BPM, Liam decided to add a catchy, uptempo, female vocal sample. It was a move he remains far from happy about.

At the time, a number of hugely successful, Europop acts such as Capella and 2 Unlimited were building entire tracks around female vocal lines.

Liam later felt that he should have done something more creative and less obviously commercial. Nevertheless, No Good (Start the Dance), featuring additional remixes by CJ Bolland and David Morley, proved not only to be a massive hit – it peaked at No. 4 in the national charts, stayed in the Top 10 for seven weeks, and eventually sold over quarter of a million copies – but also received universally good reviews.

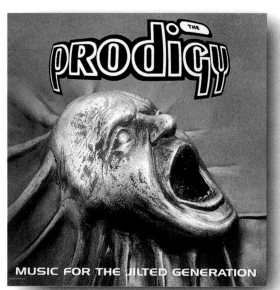

MUSIC FOR THE JILTED GENERATION

"The Prodigy don't deserve their image as tinny breakbeat-wielding chancers," reckoned Select. "No Good (Start the Dance) states their case for being at least as important as any other tattooed Techno punk. Liam Howlett's Jungle and hardcore roots are still present, but he injects some space and gracious melody between the coruscating rhythm." Already recognised as a proper band, rather than just another faceless dance act, the four members of The Prodigy now began to take on individual identities. Liam was the quiet, intense music-maker, slightly more serious than the others. Maxim was the cool, laid back MC, who oversaw the stage show through a steely stare and luminous cats'-eye contact lenses. Leeroy was the incredibly tall, chaotically graceful dancer with a unique, high-stepping style. Keith, meanwhile, began to emerge as the public face of The Prodigy. Transformed by Liam's music from a fun-loving mischief-maker into an insane, unstable mental patient, Keith, clad in chains, spiked collars and often bound inside a straitjacket, took to barking like a dog on all fours at the front of the stage, flinging himself head-first from the top of speakers into the crowd and scaring the front few rows of the audience with his expressions.

The video for No Good (Start the

What sets **Prodigy** songs apart from cheap and cheesy rave, however, is **their** **complexity** and constant change

"The **Prodigy** don't deserve their image as tinny breakbeat-wielding chancers. No Good (Start the Dance) states their case for being at least as **important** as any other tattooed **Techno** punk" Select

"
rea
wa

"Over time, the album formed a **concept** without me realising it. It came to be seen as **political.** In fact, it was all an **accident**"

Dance), shot in a disused, underground cellar below Spitalfields market in the East End of London, reinforced these individual perceptions of The Prodigy. As the cellar filled up with friends of the band, along for an illegal party, the camera concentrated in turn on Keith, Leeroy, Liam and Maxim, each expelling their excess energy in different ways: Liam, for example, was smashing a hole through a brick wall, while a fairly calm Keith suddenly went berserk.

Filmed in colour then drained to grainy black and white, the menacing, paranoid feel of the video not only suited the aggressive club vibe of the song, but also appealed to traditional music TV shows because of its narrative and high production values. According to director Walter Stern, it was trying to achieve a hard, street look, reminiscent of the spooky party sequence in the film Jacob's Ladder. Despite removing several "scenes of distress", MTV, in particular, loved the video, playing it even after the song had dropped out of the charts and vastly increasing both the band's breadth of audience and their European fan base.

In July 94, less than three years on from Charly, The Prodigy released what was to prove the most commercially successful and critically acclaimed post-Acid-House dance album to date. The band's second LP, Music for the Jilted Generation, was a powerful, energetic, euphoric and highly original amalgam of Techno, Trance, rock, funk, ambient, Hip-Hop, punk rock and heavy metal. It broke musical conventions in every genre, made hardcore club music acceptable home listening and proved that real bands didn't have to play real instruments. It made innovative use of numerous obscure samples, often chopped up into tiny fragments of a second, exploded the faceless myth of electronic music and produced Techno with as much attitude as rock'n'roll. It also entered the British and many European album charts at No. 1, went gold in under a month and eventually became the first-ever million-selling alternative dance album.

"Music for the Jilted Generation starts with a voiceover from a harassed Hollywood gangster," explained NME, who awarded the LP 9/10, "cuts into the sampled crunch of breaking glass mixed with heavy beats, and ends almost an hour later, with the voice of the Hal computer in 2001: A Space Odyssey reporting a malfunction in its semi-human mind. In between, The Prodigy show that there's no need to elaborate texts to send a message across. They just hint by way of titles, sampled voices, dialogue and a wide-ranging musical mood that fires the

"I know it sounds clichéd, but to us, the gig is a **drug** – a pure drug. We just don't need anything else. The **performance** is a narcotic"

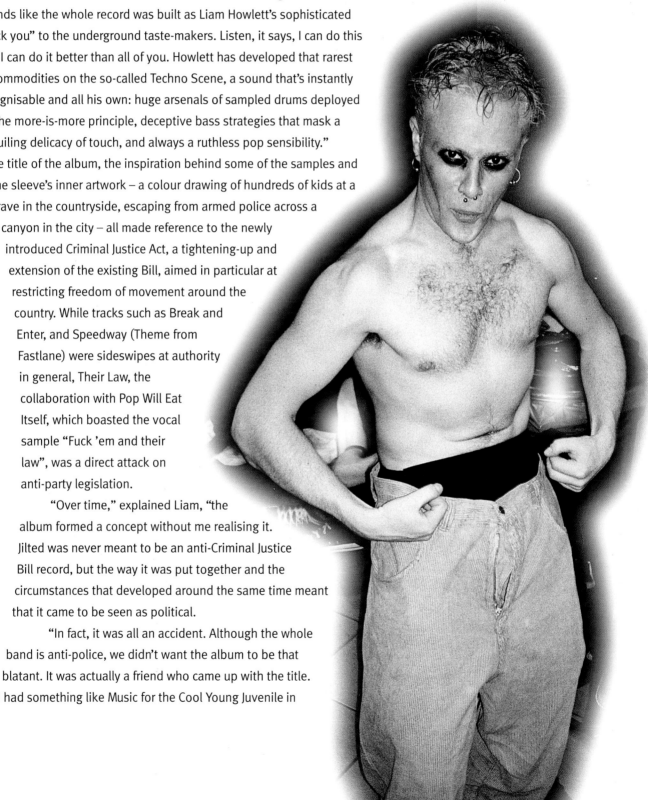

imagination. Far from being faceless and functional, there is a distinct identity here clarified by recurring motifs, juddering breakbeats, wild electronic noises and the actual shape of the tunes.

Select, who gave the album a full 5/5, stated: "Music for the Jilted Generation is possibly the best electronic pop record you'll hear this year, the instant headrush of hardcore Techno studded over with irresistible hooks and harnessed to a series of merciless grooves. It sounds like the whole record was built as Liam Howlett's sophisticated "Fuck you" to the underground taste-makers. Listen, it says, I can do this and I can do it better than all of you. Howlett has developed that rarest of commodities on the so-called Techno Scene, a sound that's instantly recognisable and all his own: huge arsenals of sampled drums deployed on the more-is-more principle, deceptive bass strategies that mask a beguiling delicacy of touch, and always a ruthless pop sensibility."

The title of the album, the inspiration behind some of the samples and the sleeve's inner artwork – a colour drawing of hundreds of kids at a rave in the countryside, escaping from armed police across a canyon in the city – all made reference to the newly introduced Criminal Justice Act, a tightening-up and extension of the existing Bill, aimed in particular at restricting freedom of movement around the country. While tracks such as Break and Enter, and Speedway (Theme from Fastlane) were sideswipes at authority in general, Their Law, the collaboration with Pop Will Eat Itself, which boasted the vocal sample "Fuck 'em and their law", was a direct attack on anti-party legislation.

"Over time," explained Liam, "the album formed a concept without me realising it. Jilted was never meant to be an anti-Criminal Justice Bill record, but the way it was put together and the circumstances that developed around the same time meant that it came to be seen as political.

"In fact, it was all an accident. Although the whole band is anti-police, we didn't want the album to be that blatant. It was actually a friend who came up with the title. I had something like Music for the Cool Young Juvenile in mind, or Music for Joyriders maybe, but neither of them worked.

"I am very wary of being held up as a spokesman. None of the band want to step on stage and go, "Fuck the police," like NWA or something. I would prefer The Prodigy to represent the very opposite of a politicised stance. We are about making good, hard dance music that people can listen to and forget all their troubles, forget politics and just enjoy themselves."

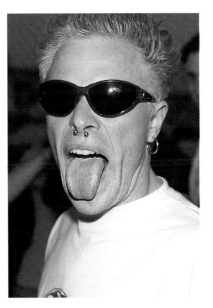

In fact, while all of the band frequently voiced their objections to sections of the Criminal Justice Act, which stopped even small groups of people gathering together, restricted access to public property and allowed the police to stop and search without cause, they were also careful to distance themselves from other laws with which they felt no grievance. For example, Liam stated publicly that reducing the rights of squatters and travellers was of no interest to him since it bore no relation to his own life. He even suggested that proposals to widen motorways through the English countryside would be a good idea if it helped him to get to London more quickly.

"Liam Howlett does not want to be a spokesman for his generation, but, by default, he's ended up as a spokesman for degeneration," concluded NME. "He is a frontline reporter sending eye-witness accounts from the war between the authorities and Britain's multi-hued youth. He's a Robocop and a modern-day Beethoven rolled into one."

Music for the Jilted Generation remained in the UK Top 20 for four months after its release, despite receiving almost no commercial radio play. Unlike Experience, which was peculiarly British in its extreme use of breakbeats, it also continued to sell well across Europe, marking up its first sales before the end of the year.

As the band's commercial success continued to escalate, their shows became wilder, and their music and image more rock'n'roll. For the first time, The Prodigy found themselves being taken as seriously as more purist dance acts, such as Orbital and Aphex Twin. So, since Orbital were headlining the second stage at that year's Glastonbury festival, the band decided to ask the organisers if they, too, could perform. They were refused.

"We were told we weren't big enough," Liam later admitted to Blah Blah Blah. "We just wanted to take part. We offered to do it for free, even pay our own expenses, but they preferred to bore the audience with some

so-called cool bands. That really annoyed me. If people want to see a nice light show, they can go to the Planetarium. I don't like putting other bands down, but you'd have to be on about 30 mushrooms and at least a couple of Acid to have fun watching that."

Nevertheless, The Prodigy were now averaging one show every four days. While promoting the album, they performed to more than 300,000 people in 25 different countries. Notably, they were appearing at European festivals such as the Feile in Ireland, alongside a variety of styles of bands such as the Red Hot Chili Peppers, and also playing gigs in huge, outdoor arenas usually booked by rock groups. The Prodigy, however, were not neglecting their dance roots. They travelled to Japan where they played to thousands of fans, even though the event turned out to be a fake rave, featuring performances by both Capella and 2 Unlimited. The band also joined the likes of Underworld, Sasha, Carl Cox and

Laurent Garnier for a Universe party at a disused airport in Munich, which attracted more than 20,000 people.

"The Prodigy show in Munich is a killer," reported NME. "A pantomime of Speed dementia, Keith comes on in a straitjacket and heads for the crowd, spitting water, lolling his tongue and dancing like an Alice Cooper amphetamine nightmare. Leeroy spins and bends on invisible strings. Maxim screams with enough method seriousness to have his satanic contact lenses bulging. And Liam, walled in by keyboard tech at the back, lunges at his gear, concussive breakbeats and barbed sonic squalls tearing into the crowd. Despite dropping in the slower Hip-Hop of Poison and the sugared pop hook of No Good (Start the Dance), it's basically a blistering hardcore show. Pure acceleration. Pure brain-booting aggression."

"I think a certain type of person buys our records," noted Liam at the time. "If you take a Capella song and a Prodigy song, the Prodigy track will be much nastier-sounding. And that's exactly where we're from. I'm into any music that has a bit of aggression, really."

In the same month as the Munich show, The Prodigy received their biggest acknowledgment to date from the established UK music industry when Music for the Jilted Generation was one of 10 albums nominated for the prestigious Mercury Music Award. Despite losing out in the end to soft, soul-pop outfit M People, Liam was surprisingly pleased with the nomination.

"That we were even included is good enough for me," he told NME, "because all the other bands there went through the normal route. The likes of Blur, M People and Therapy? were all supported and played on the radio. We weren't, and I think that's a good thing. I'm not trying to say it's a purer form of a certain scene. It's just that we've managed to get there in a different way."

The only snag in The Prodigy's phenomenal success was the collapse of their American record deal. Only one month after Music for the Jilted Generation had topped the British charts, Elektra dropped the band. Following negligible sales of Experience and the subsequent, loss-making US tour, the label insisted that Liam rerecord tracks for the US market to make them more mainstream. The final straw came when they deemed One Love too extreme to release at all, despite being one of the most accessible tracks on Music for the Jilted Generation.

Meanwhile, The Prodigy continued to tour and, in August, released a third single from the album, Voodoo People, a fast, flute-infested mix of tribal rhythms and percussive House.

"This guitar-powered piece of voodoo should turn your floor into a gurning, throbbing mass of happy faces," reckoned Mixmag Update. "It's as

"I am very wary of being held up as a **spokesman**. None of the band wants to step on stage and go, '**Fuck** the police,' like NWA or something. I would prefer **The Prodigy** to represent the very opposite of a politicised stance. We are about making **good**, hard **dance** music that people can listen to and forget all their troubles, forget politics and just **enjoy** themselves" – Liam

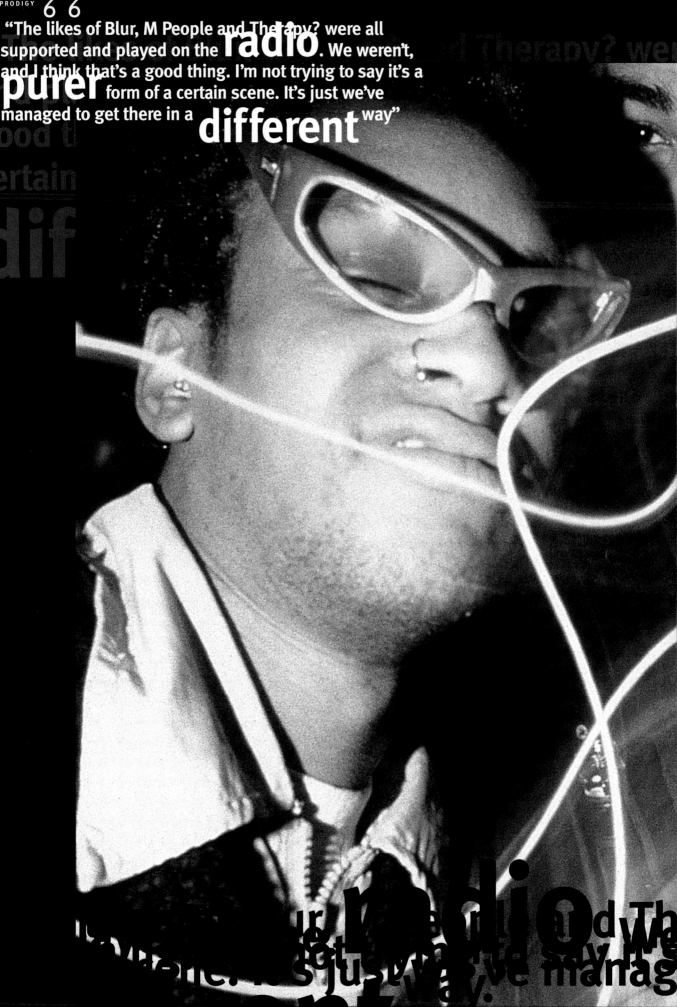

"The likes of Blur, M People and Therapy? were all supported and played on the **radio**. We weren't, and I think that's a good thing. I'm not trying to say it's a **purer** form of a certain scene. It's just we've managed to get there in a **different** way"

all supported

pure

all supported

to get there in a

large as they come: big, burning and powerful, with a million tons of oomph, piles of dynamic percussion and a killer guitar riff. It's also, I reckon, the best thing they've ever done."

Also boasting a superb Dust Brothers remix, Voodoo People, with its "Voodoo who do what you don't dare do" sample, became a No. 12 hit. The single may well be best remembered, however, for its lavish, tropical video. Filmed on the exotic Caribbean island of St Lucia, it continued to focus individually on all four members of the band, who were playing out a narrative about being chased by a witch doctor. Even the unhinged antics in the video, however, failed to match The Prodigy's by now spectacularly theatrical gigs. Forsaking his straitjacket for a smoke-filled glass box, from which he would try frantically to escape,

Keith remained the visual focus of the show, while above the stage, a suspended screen flashed up random, psychedelic images and laser lights beamed across the crowd. For the first time, another musician appeared on stage with the band – a guitarist.

Reviewing the London show of the band's Voodoo People tour, Vox said: "Tonight is nothing less than the full-on, frenzied chaos of a hardcore rave. And that's just how The Prodigy like it. Their albums may be uncompromising but, live, their sound is twice as aggressive. Familiar snatches of former Top 20 singles slip seamlessly into a powerful hour of Jungle, Techno, Trance, heavy House and Hip-Hop. A deep bass anchors every beat, while infectiously simple samples add the perfect pop touch.

"What sets The Prodigy's songs apart from cheap and cheesy rave, however, is their complexity and constant change. Unlike almost all electronic hardcore, the relentless, repetitive, speedy beats are never allowed to become monotonous. Liam is clearly in control, maintaining the engaging, hypnotic pace and incessantly progressing the sounds and samples to hold the audience's attention. The effect is pure paranoia, an all-encompassing confusion from which there seems

no escape. The volume, recurring references to voodoo and sheer severity of the music combine to create an almost evil force. There is more black magic to The Prodigy than any death-metal band could muster."

So extreme were the shows that Keith began to throw up regularly both before and during the set, simply because of the adrenalin rush of excitement. "I know it sounds clichéd," he confessed, "but to us the gig is a drug – a pure drug. We just don't need anything else. The performance is a narcotic."

"I'm not The Prodigy," Liam then stated to Select. "People see me as the whole band, but we'd never have sold all those records without the live show. This is a band of the 90s, where you don't need real instruments, but you still get that feel of a gang, where everybody has their role. If I got a few more dancers, the music would be the same, but it would not be The Prodigy anymore."

The critics – even those usually obsessed with rock and indie music – were forced to agree. The Prodigy ended 1994 with a new press moniker: The Best Rock'n'Roll Band in Britain.

If you take a Capella song and a **Prodigy** song, the Prodigy track will be much **nastier**-sounding. And that's exactly where we're from. I'm into any music that has a bit of **aggression**, really

chapter six

Post-

Mercury Award nomination, The Prodigy's new-found status as a so-called proper band brought about a shift in their public profile. Fans and the media alike wanted to know as much about the personalities and private lives of the band as they did about the songs themselves. Such a concept sat uneasily with The Prodigy, who had always shunned the celebrity element to making music, and who continued to court the respect of the dance community.

"Since we've had a lot of commercial success, it's hard to convince people we're not pop stars," Liam tried to explain to NME. "Our records are in the charts, but that's it. I mean, would you say Ice Cube has sold out? We'll never sell out to anyone. The worst thing is to sell out to yourself, and if I was to write songs I wasn't into, that would be letting myself down as well as the people who are into the band. Mind you, I'm starting to think I worry too much about trying to be credible and underground."

Liam later told Melody Maker: "I guess I'm just afraid of totally, totally crossing over. I want to keep one foot in the underground. I want to be respected. Maybe I make it into more of a problem than it is. As we go down the line, every record is going to get harder for us. If I could sell a set amount every time, say 100,000 copies, and stick at that level, that's what I'd prefer. With every new tune, we have to fight to constantly prove what we do. People don't understand because all they see is us on MTV. That's why we have to set ourselves apart from other commercial bands." The habits of all four of The Prodigy became the new focus for the media, in particular, those that were seen to influence the attitude of the band: their growing interest in buzz sports such as snowboarding and parachuting, for example, or their passion for motorbikes and fast cars. Liam had long since swapped his Ford Cortina for a Mercedes Sport, then a Cosworth Escort and an AC Cobra.

"I'm a bit of a speed freak," he confessed to NME. "The fastest I've ever been was on the back of Keith's bike. He must have been doing around 160mph. I get a buzz out of being that close to death. Actually, that was a bit nasty. I thought I was definitely dying.

"I'm really surprised that I haven't been caught speeding myself. I'm not a maniac, but I used to go out at night and drive stupid speeds. I'm not a boy racer by any means, but I've always been into that power burst. It's a bit like the film Point Break. That movie sums us up as a band, really."

In March 95, having just picked up awards for Best Dance-Act of 94 from both MTV and NME, Best Live Band from Muzik magazine and Best Dance album at the Independent Dance Awards, The Prodigy released Poison, the fourth and

We'll never sell out to anyone. The worst thing is to sell out to yourself

songs

"The worst thing is to **sell** out to yourself and if I was to write songs I wasn't into, that would be letting myself **down** as well as the people who are into the band."

"Since we've had a lot of **commercial** success, it's hard to convince people we're not **pop** stars"

Si we've had a lot of convince people w

comurcial success
e're ho up ars

"I want to keep one foot in the **underground**. I want to be respected. As we go down the line, every record is going to get **harder** for us"

Imagine if this band had guitar riffs you could beat your granny to **death** with, and they could get absolutely everyone in the audience dancing like their boots were on fire. Believe it or not, you are imagining **The Prodigy**

"The **live** act is what we're all about. We've dedicated the past five years of our lives to it, so we don't just want a polite round of applause at the end of a show. We want to stir people up so much that they have to be carried out, **exhausted**, on a stretcher" – Keith

The Prodigy spent the rest of the summer playing scores of outdoor festivals in the UK and across central Europe, as well as in Russia, Macedonia, Romania, Israel and America. The sheer number of people who witnessed their stunning shows, combined with TV coverage of the events, saw the band swell their fan base to stadium-size within the space of six months, and without even releasing a record. Over one memorable weekend in August, The Prodigy played Glasgow's T in the Park on Friday night, Ireland's Feile Festival on the Saturday and, at around midnight on Sunday, they put in a headlining appearance at Iceland's Uxi event. All three gigs were spectacularly received and, even on the final night, the band put in a characteristically energetic performance. At the Lollipop festival in Sweden, Keith took to the stage with the Chemical Brothers, who later admitted they would never be able to get their own dancers, since nobody could possibly match Keith's antics.

In October, The Prodigy played a 1,000-capacity home gig at Ilford's The Island in Essex. Metal mag Kerrang! reviewed the show, awarding it 5/5.

"Drop, if you will, all those daft musical prejudices and imagine a band so loud that the bass shakes a layer of dust down from the ceiling. Imagine if this band had guitar riffs you could beat your granny to death with and they could get absolutely everyone in the audience dancing like their boots were on fire. Believe it or not, you are imagining The Prodigy. There were moments tonight when this band could have scared Satan. A few years back, there was debate as to whether Kerrang! should write about grunge or not. We did, and the world didn't blow up. The Prodigy won't blow the world up either, but they'll definitely blow your mind. Prodigy are the best band in the UK."

The Ilford show also saw The Prodigy introduce their most extreme visual style to date. Punk-influenced piercings took their body adornment one step further. While Liam and Maxim joined Keith in getting their noses pierced, both stopped short of his stud through the tongue. Keith also took to dying his hair technicolour: at The Island, it was purple and yellow.

"I don't know if my hair's falling out or anything," he told Select, "but it's fun. The different reactions from people are mad. Some old ladies say how nice it is – one told me I looked like an exotic bird that had escaped from an aviary. Others think they're your parents, and stick their nose in the air. But it's my first taste of prejudice and I love it."

The Prodigy ended 95 with a British tour of indoor rock venues. For the first time, their gigs were reviewed in the mainstream daily press. The Times watched the Brixton Academy show.

"When the sound of The Sex Pistols' Anarchy in the UK came blasting over the house PA, directly before The Prodigy took to the stage, it acted as both an aural incendiary device and a statement of intent. There is nothing cerebral about The Prodigy's particular type of dance music, which seems to work on the same principle as heavy metal: turn it on, turn it up and keep it going. In among the biggest crowd-pleasers from last year's Music for the Jilted Generation album, they played their forthcoming single, Firestarter, which featured Keith on vocals, and proved that The

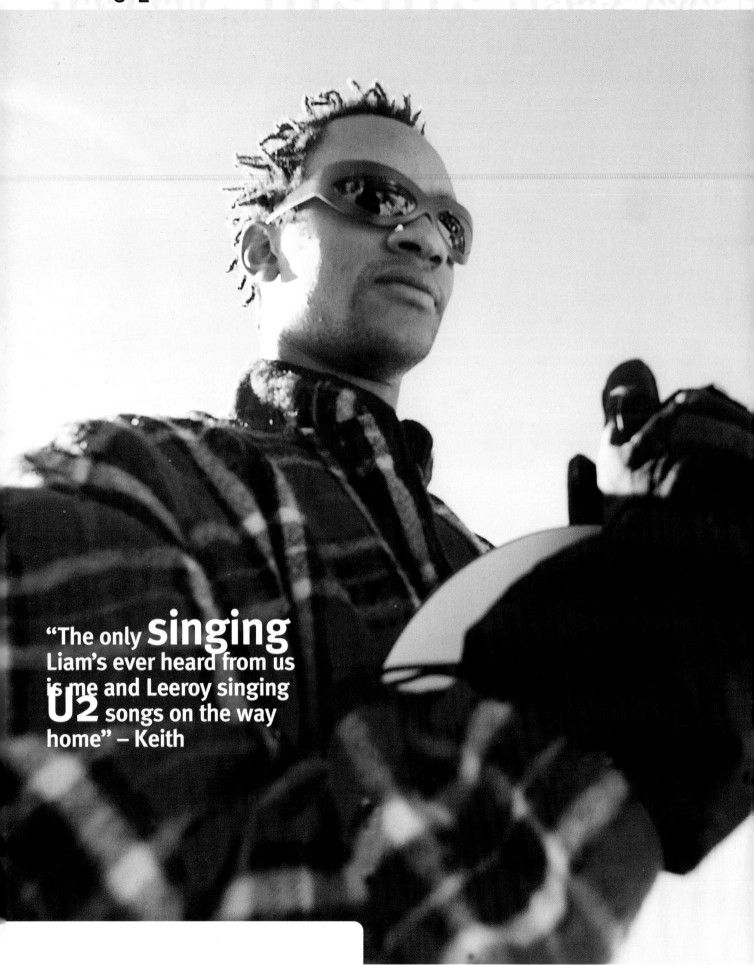

"The only **singing** Liam's ever heard from us is me and Leeroy singing **U2** songs on the way home" – Keith

Prodigy are no longer just an incredibly popular dance band – they're fast becoming one of the heaviest bands in the country."

In fact, Firestarter, which had long been scheduled for early January, did not come out until mid-March. With The Prodigy's heavy touring schedule, Liam, who was supposed to be writing material for the new album over the winter, turned out to have spent his spare time snowboarding. It had, he explained, become his pressure release, just like dancing on stage was the rest of the band's.

In the end, The Prodigy spent the first month of the year in Australia. They joined Tricky, Rage Against the Machine, Porno for Pyros and Nick Cave as headliners of the Big Day Out, the Antipodean equivalent of American touring festival Lollapolooza. The following month, the band were guests on the first show of Channel 4's snowboarding series Boardstupid, and disappeared to Switzerland for filming. By the time Firestarter was ready to be released, Liam had completed just four songs for the new album. In an interview with Blah Blah Blah, he described them as similar to the slower Hip-Hop of Poison.

"There's definitely more attitude coming through in the music," he said. "It's still hard, but there's not as many big breakdowns. I'm constantly coming across tunes that give me inspiration. That's why I'm always out and about watching bands at festivals. The only pressure on me now is to progress the music. I want to surprise people every time a Prodigy record comes out. That's what I'm thinking while I write."

Liam also talked about his writing process to The Face. "I like to think of myself as a half-hearted songwriter," he declared. "I don't want to write whole songs because The Prodigy is still a dance band, although we've sure more songs than the average dance band. When people like Jesus Jones have tried to blend the two before, it's never convincing. We're right in the middle, between rock music and dance music."

Liam also invited The Face to his home studio to play them tracks from the new album, including Come Correct, Rock'n'Roll and the Beastie Boys sampling Funky Shit, all of which had been part of the band's live set for several months. When Select later visited the same studio, they noticed some of the albums Liam had been listening to: Ravemania: The First Generation, Rotterdam Techno Is Hard Hard Hard, as well as Supergrass, Oasis and Skunk Anansie. It was Firestarter, however, which caught every critic's attention.

Punk vocals by Keith were mixed with samples from The Breeders and The Art of Noise and laid over metallic Hip-Hop rhythms to create a chaotic, infectious hardcore frenzy. In the third week of March 1996, Firestarter entered the British charts at No. 1, where it would stay for an entire month, finally selling more than half a million copies. "To most people," Liam told

"What's a **firestarter**? Isn't that obvious?
It's **Keith** – it's his personality"

Blah Blah Blah, "Keith is just that mad bloke who has been wiggling his legs about on stage for the last five years. Now he's had a go at some lyrics. It actually came about by accident. Firestarter was already a good instrumental track, but I knew it was missing the usual Prodigy hook that sticks in your head. Keith came into the studio, said he'd like to try singing on it and went away and wrote some words. What's a firestarter? Isn't that obvious? It's Keith – it's his personality."

"We had no idea how it was going to sound," Keith admitted to NME, "because the only singing Liam's ever heard from us is me and Leeroy singing U2 songs on the way home. We always harmonise on One, but instead of cigarette lighters, we turn on our mobile phones and wave them in the air."

For once, The Prodigy's refusal to play Top of the Pops proved a major problem. The band took off to Colorado to snowboard, to celebrate their success, while TV shows were forced to screen the video, a menacing, black and white adventure story filmed in the tunnel of a disused London Underground station amid clouds of choking dust.

Subsequently, the programme received its biggest number of complaints ever. Parents phoned in to say that the sight of Keith was frightening their children, while the BBC later invited viewers on to a talk show to discuss how distressing the entire episode had been. Without doubt, Firestarter had caught the attention of the nation and proved to be an invaluable antidote to boring Britpop. Manic Street Preachers guitarist Nicky Wire appeared in Melody Maker wearing a Prodigy T-shirt, The Sunday Times asked the band to name their Top 10 LPs of all time, New Order and Electronic singer Bernard Sumner called them the best new band in Britain and the Smashing Pumpkins – one of Liam's all-time favourite bands – covered Firestarter on their UK tour. Liam, meanwhile, was progressing quickly with the remainder of the album. At The Prodigy's first British concert of the year, headlining the dance day at Brighton's Essential Music Festival, the band showcased several new songs. They opened with a Hip-Hop track, tentatively titled Smack My Bitch Up, which mutated midway through into a Middle Eastern Sheila Chandra vocal sample. They then played the by-now-familiar Funky Shit and Rock'n'Roll. Another brand new song, Breathe, boasting a James Bond/John Barry synth riff, saw Keith and Maxim duelling on vocals for the first time. Finally came the instantly addictive Minefields, the track scheduled to be The Prodigy's follow-up to Firestarter until the band decided to put out only the album. In the studio, Liam had also almost completed a further two tracks. One, called Diesel Power, was a Mission: Impossible-style song featuring Ultramagnetic MCs rapper Kool Keith on vocals. The other brought in Skunk Anansie's astonishing frontwoman, Skin. In their final piece of press prior to both the release of the

"I'm constantly coming across tunes that give me **inspiration.** That's why I'm always out and about watching bands at **festivals.** The only pressure on me now is to **progress** the music. I want to surprise people every time a Prodigy record comes out" – Liam

album and the band's appearance at every major UK summer festival – a Face cover story featuring a photo of Keith screaming from the front page – Liam contemplated the future for The Prodigy.

"I didn't really expect Firestarter to be accepted so well," he confessed. "I thought people wouldn't get into it because of the guitars. I'd love to put out another song like that, but it's always in the back of my head that people will start to think we're a guitar band now, that we're leaving our old thing behind. We've always said that we don't want to be a Techno band."

What kind of band do you want to be, then? "We want to be an alternative dance band with energy. It's quite obvious we're not a club band anymore, but we don't want to give up writing good dance music and start writing dodgy rock'n'roll. That just happens to be the energy we're interested in at the moment. Ultimately, I want to create something more anarchic."

Currently, however, Liam's main ambition is to break The Prodigy in America. Keith's ambition – naturally – is a little more convoluted.

"The real challenge for The Prodigy now," he maintains, "is to rock people who think they don't want to be rocked. Before I was in this band, I used to hang out with a bunch of strict metalheads. We'd go to real rock venues and if I danced, I was dissed. You could smoke a ton of draw, drink 14 Special Brews and fall over, but if you shuffled your feet, that was the end of you. Now metalheads come to our concerts and don't notice they're not listening to traditional music. They start moving around without even realising. Suddenly they're like, 'Oh my God, what am I doing? I'm dancing!' That's precisely what The Prodigy will always be about."

"I didn't really expect **Firestarter** to be accepted so well. I thought people wouldn't get into it because of the **guitars**. We've always said that we don't want to be a **Techno** band" – Liam

guitars expect Firestarter We've always said that we always said that we don't want to b

e accepted so well. I thought people wouldn
it want to be a Tec
won't I thought
a techno

al challenge for the now, of strict metalheads. We'd go to rea drink 14 Special Brews and fall over but if of your feet. That was the end of you. Now metal itional music. They start moving around ealising. Suddenly they're like, Oh my God, wha I'm dancing. That's precisely what The Prodigy s be about" – Keith

"The real challenge for The **Prodigy** now," he maintains, "is to **rock** people who think they don't want to be rocked. Before I was in this band, I used to hang out with a bunch of strict **metalheads.** We'd go to real rock venues and if I danced, I was dissed. You could smoke a ton of draw, drink 14 **Special Brews** and fall over, but if you shuffled your feet, that was the end of you. Now metalheads come to our concerts and don't notice they're not listening to **traditional** music. They start moving around without even realising. Suddenly, they're like, 'Oh my God, what am I doing? I'm dancing!' That's precisely what The Prodigy will always be about" – Keith

to be
a
ock
on of
ds
to
nput

discography

SINGLES

FEBRUARY 1991	WHAT EVIL LURKS
AUGUST 1991	CHARLY
DECEMBER 1991	EVERYBODY IN THE PLACE
SEPTEMBER 1992	FIRE
NOVEMBER 1992	OUT OF SPACE
MARCH 1993	WIND IT UP
OCTOBER 1993	ONE LOVE
MAY 1994	NO GOOD (START THE DANCE)
AUGUST 1994	VOODOO PEOPLE
MARCH 1995	POISON
FEBRUARY 1996	FIRESTARTER

ALBUMS

NOVEMBER 1992	EXPERIENCE
JULY 1994	MUSIC FOR THE JILTED GENERATION

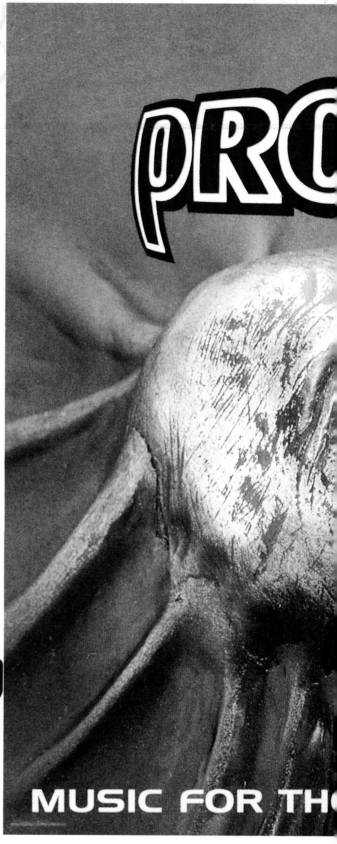

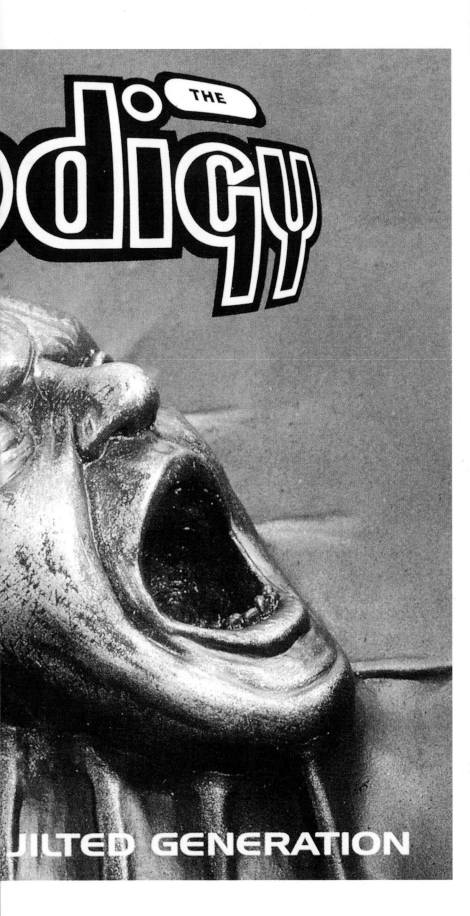

JILTED GENERATION

the prodigy

exit the underground

Photographs: Rip/Pat Pope/All Action/Rex Features/Retna/Davis and Davis/Phil Nichols/SIN/Redferns/Motorcycle News

Text : Lisa Verrico

Design : Brett Lewis

Printed in Italy